***Issues in Religion an***

1

The Messianic Secret

## *Issues in Religion and Theology*



***Titles in the series include:***

1 The Messianic Secret *ed. Christopher Tuckett*

2 Visionaries and their Apocalypses *ed. Paul D. Hanson*

3 The Interpretation of Matthew *ed. Graham Stanton*

4 Theodicy in the Old Testament *ed. James L. Crenshaw*

*Issues in Religion and Theology 1*

# The Messianic Secret

*Edited with an Introduction by*

CHRISTOPHER TUCKETT

FORTRESS PRESS | SPCK
Philadelphia | London

First published in Great Britain 1983
SPCK
Holy Trinity Church
Marylebone Road
London NW1 4DU

First published in the USA 1983
Fortress Press
2900 Queen Lane
Philadelphia
Pennsylvania 19129



**Library of Congress Cataloging in Publication Data**
Main entry under title:

The Messianic secret.

(Issues in religion and theology; 1)
Reprint of articles originally published 1958–1976.
Bibliography: p.
Includes index.
Contents: Introduction/Christopher Tuckett—The purpose of Mark's Gospel/Nils Alstrup Dahl—The blindness of the disciples in Mark/Joseph B. Tyson—[etc.]
1. Messianic secret (Bible)—Addresses, essays, lectures. 2. Bible. N. T. Mark—Criticism, interpretation, etc.—Addresses, essays, lectures. I. Tuckett, C. M. (Christopher Mark) II, Series.
BT245.M47 1983 226′.306 83–5499
ISBN 0–8006–1767–3

**British Library Cataloguing in Publication Data**
The Messianic secret.—(Issues in religion and theology; no. 1)
1. Bible N.T. Mark 2. Messianic secret (Bible)
I. Tuckett, Christopher II. Series
226′.306 BS2585.2

ISBN 0–281–04052–4

Filmset by Northumberland Press Ltd, Gateshead
Printed in Great Britain by Richard Clay (The Chaucer Press) Ltd,
Bungay, Suffolk

# Contents

# Acknowledgements

Nils Alstrup Dahl, "The Purpose of Mark's Gospel" is reprinted by permission from *Jesus in the Memory of the Early Church* (Minneapolis: Augsburg, 1976) 55–60. Copyright © Augsburg Publishing House 1976.

Joseph B. Tyson, "The Blindness of the Disciples in Mark" is reprinted from the *Journal of Biblical Literature* 80 (1961) 261–8 by permission of the author and *JBL*. Copyright © *Journal of Biblical Literature* 1961.

T. Alec Burkill, "Mysterious Revelation" is reprinted by permission from *Mysterious Revelation: An Examination of the Philosophy of St Mark's Gospel* (New York: Cornell University Press, 1963) 319–24. Copyright © Cornell University Press 1963.

Georg Strecker, "The Theory of the Messianic Secret in Mark's Gospel" is reprinted by permission of *Studia Evangelica* and the author. Original publication as "Zur Messiasgeheimnistheorie im Markusevangelium" in *Studia Evangelica* 3, TU 88 (1964) 87–104. Copyright © Georg Strecker 1964.

Eduard Schweizer, "The Question of the Messianic Secret in Mark" is reprinted by permission of the author. Original publication as "Zur Messiasgeheimnis bei Markus" in *Zeitschrift für die neutestamentliche Wissenschaft* 56 (1965) 1–8. Copyright © Eduard Schweizer 1965.

Ulrich Luz, "The Secrecy Motif and the Marcan Christology" is reprinted by permission of the author. Original publication as "Das Geheimnismotiv und die Markinische Christologie" in *Zeitschrift für die neutestamentliche Wissenschaft* 56 (1965) 9–30. Copyright © Ulrich Luz 1965.

William C. Robinson Jr, "The Quest for Wrede's Secret Messiah" is reprinted by permission of the Union Theological Seminary. Original publication in *Interpretation* 27 (1973) 10–30. Copyright © Union Theological Seminary 1973.

James D. G. Dunn, "The Messianic Secret in Mark" is reprinted by permission of Inter-Varsity Press. Original publication in the *Tyndale Bulletin* 21 (1970) 92–117 (reprinted, slightly abbreviated, in the *TSF Bulletin* (Summer 1974) 7–14). Copyright © Inter-Varsity Press 1970.

Heikki Räisänen, "The 'Messianic Secret' in Mark's Gospel" is reprinted by permission from *Das "Messiasgeheimnis" im Markusevangelium* (Helsinki: Lansi-Suomi, 1976) 159–68. Copyright © E. J. Brill 1976.

# *The Contributors*

CHRISTOPHER TUCKETT is Lecturer in New Testament Studies at the University of Manchester. He is the author of *The Revival of the Griesbach Hypothesis* (1983) and a frequent contributor to journals of biblical scholarship.

NILS ALSTRUP DAHL is Emeritus Professor of New Testament at the Yale University Divinity School. His *Das Volk Gottes* was published in 1941. Three volumes of his essays have now been translated into English: *The Crucified Messiah* (1974), *Jesus in the Memory of the Early Church* (1976) and *Studies in Paul* (1977).

JOSEPH B. TYSON is Professor of Religious Studies at the Southern Methodist University, Dallas, Texas. He is the author of *A Study of Early Christianity* (1973), and is a regular contributor to theological journals.

T. ALEC BURKILL was until his retirement Professor of Religious Studies at the University of Zimbabwe. In addition to *Mysterious Revelation* (1963), he has published another collection of essays on Mark's Gospel, *New Light on the Earliest Gospel* (1972).

GEORG STRECKER is Professor of New Testament Studies at the University of Göttingen. He is the author of *Das Judenchristentum in den Pseudoklementinen* (1958), *Der Weg der Gerechtigkeit* (1962) and a volume of essays, *Eschaton und Historie* (1979).

EDUARD SCHWEIZER was Professor of New Testament Theology and Exegesis at the University of Zürich from 1949 to 1978. A number of his books have been translated, including his commentaries, *The Good News according to Mark* (1971), *The Good News according to Matthew* (1976) and *The Letter to the Colossians* (1982).

ULRICH LUZ is Professor of New Testament Studies at the University of Berne. After a period as *Assistent* to Eduard Schweizer in Zürich, he held a Chair at the University of Göttingen for several years. His *Das Geschichtsverständnis des Paulus* was published in 1968, and a major commentary on Matthew is forthcoming.

WILLIAM C. ROBINSON JR is Taylor Professor of Biblical Theology and History at Andover Newton Theological School. He is the author of a study of Luke's theology, *Der Weg des Herrn* (1964) and a contributor to journals of biblical scholarship.

JAMES D. G. DUNN is Professor of Divinity in the University of Durham. He is the author of *Baptism in the Holy Spirit* (1970), *Jesus and the Spirit* (1975), *Unity and Diversity in the New Testament* (1977) and *Christology in the Making* (1981).

HEIKKI RÄISÄNEN is Professor of New Testament Exegesis in the University of Helsinki. In addition to *Das Messiasgeheimnis im Markusevangelium* (1976), he has published another study of Mark's Gospel, *Die Parabeltheorie im Markusevangelium* (1973) and several articles on Paul.

# Series Foreword

The "Issues in Religion and Theology" series intends to encompass a variety of topics within the general disciplines of religious and theological studies. Subjects are drawn from any of the component fields, such as biblical studies, systematic theology, ethics, history of Christian thought, and history of religion. The issues have all proved to be highly significant for their respective areas, and they are of similar interest to students, teachers, clergy, and general readers.

The series aims to address these issues by collecting and reproducing key studies, all previously published, which have contributed significantly to our present understandings. In each case, the volume editor introduces the discussion with an original essay which describes the subject and its treatment in religious and theological studies. To this editor has also fallen the responsibility of selecting items for inclusion – no easy task when one considers the vast number of possibilities. Together the essays are intended to present a balanced overview of the problem and various approaches to it. Each piece is important in the current debate, and any older publication included normally stands as a "classical" or seminal work which is still worth careful study. Readers unfamiliar with the issue should find that these discussions provide a good entrée, while more advanced students will appreciate having studies by some of the best specialists on the subject gathered together in one volume. The editor has, of course, faced certain constraints: analyses too lengthy or too technical could not be included, except perhaps in excerpt form; the bibliography is not exhaustive; and the volumes in this series are being kept to a reasonable, uniform length. On the other hand, the editor is able to overcome the real problem of inaccessibility. Much of the best literature on a subject is often not readily available to readers, whether because it was first published in journals or books not widely circulated or because it was originally written in a language not read by all who would benefit from it. By bringing these and other studies together in this series, we hope to contribute to the general understanding of these key topics.

The series editors and the publishers wish to express their gratitude to the authors and their original publishers whose works are reprinted or translated here, often with corrections from living authors. We are also conscious of our debt to members of the editorial advisory board. They have shared our belief that the series will be useful on a wide scale, and they have therefore been prepared to spare much time and thought for the project.

DOUGLAS A. KNIGHT
ROBERT MORGAN

# *Abbreviations*

| | |
|---|---|
| *BJRL* | *Bulletin of the John Rylands Library* |
| *CBQ* | *Catholic Biblical Quarterly* |
| *ET* | English translation/English translator |
| *EvQ* | *Evangelical Quarterly* |
| *EvT* | *Evangelische Theologie* |
| *ExpTim* | *Expository Times* |
| *HTR* | *Harvard Theological Review* |
| *Int* | *Interpretation* |
| *JBL* | *Journal of Biblical Literature* |
| *JSOT* | *Journal for the Study of the Old Testament* |
| *JTS* | *Journal of Theological Studies* |
| *NovT* | *Novum Testamentum* |
| *NTS* | *New Testament Studies* |
| *RB* | *Revue Biblique* |
| *RGG* | *Religion in Geschichte und Gegenwart* |
| *SE* | *Studia Evangelica* |
| *TDNT* | G. Kittel and G. Friedrich (ed.), *Theological Dictionary of the New Testament* |
| *TLZ* | *Theologische Literaturzeitung* |
| TU | Texte und Untersuchungen |
| *TynBul* | *Tyndale Bulletin* |
| *ZNW* | *Zeitschrift für die neutestamentliche Wissenschaft* |
| *ZTK* | *Zeitschrift für Theologie und Kirche* |

# *Introduction*
# *The Problem of the Messianic Secret*

CHRISTOPHER TUCKETT

It is a well-known feature of the gospel tradition, especially of the Gospel of Mark, that Jesus is frequently portrayed as seeking to maintain an element of secrecy about his own person and work. This feature is usually known today as the "messianic secret", a term which derives from W. Wrede's classic study of this aspect of the Gospels.[1] As a result of this work, Wrede has been described as the forerunner of form criticism and redaction criticism,[2] and in terms of method, the influence of his book has continued right up to the present day.[3] However, the details of some of his individual arguments are now questioned, and with regard to the messianic secret itself, there is still no unanimity about its correct interpretation.[4] It seems therefore desirable to set the various views represented in this collection of essays in context by giving a brief history of research into the messianic secret.[5]

Prior to Wrede's work, few nineteenth-century critics had seen any difficulties in using the Gospels to rediscover an earthly Jesus, unencumbered by later ecclesiastical dogma. The earlier studies of Holtzmann and others[6] had convinced the majority of scholars of the literary priority of Mark's Gospel. However, this was then often taken as an indication of Mark's historical reliability.[7] In particular, discussion of the secrecy texts in Mark was assumed to concern only the historical question of why Jesus might have enjoined secrecy on others. The most frequent answer was that Jesus was seeking to avoid popular ideas of messiahship with their political overtones. A number of "lives of Jesus" were written, all based for their chronology on the Marcan outline, and many of these centred on the idea of Jesus' gradual revelation to others of his own basic conviction that he was the Messiah. Jesus became conscious that he was the Messiah at his baptism, but in the first stage of his ministry he kept this secret. When the demoniacs recognized him, Jesus ordered them not to spread their knowledge to others so that the correct evaluation of his person might develop gradually in peoples' minds. Slowly the disciples did become aware of Jesus' true identity, this growth in understanding reaching its climax in Peter's confession at Caesarea Philippi. This marked a great turning point in Jesus' ministry, and inaugurated a new period when Jesus had to try to free the disciples from Jewish nationalistic ideas of messiahship and to teach them about the necessity of his suffering. Jesus still kept his identity hidden from the crowds until his miracles led to public recognition (cf. Mark 10:47), and finally Jesus accepted the crowds' acclamation of him as the messianic king at the entry into Jerusalem. Jesus acknowledged his messiahship publicly before the high priest and was crucified as "King of the Jews".[8]

Basic to this type of reconstruction is the idea of development, with a chronology very heavily dependent on Mark's account. Some of the weaknesses and inadequacies of these "lives" were devastatingly exposed by A. Schweitzer in his magisterial survey, *The Quest of the Historical Jesus*. Schweitzer showed how much each author had read into his reconstruction details which were not there in the Gospels, and in doing so had made a Jesus in his own image. Schweitzer's fundamental criticism of these reconstructions was that they failed to take seriously the vital element in Jesus' life, viz. eschatology. Eschatology was not a dispensable "husk" which could be discarded to get back to a true "kernel" of Jesus' teaching about the universal fatherhood of God. Rather, Jesus was a strange figure of first-century Judaism whose life was dominated by the belief that the final, eschatological events were about to break in and bring an end to the present world order. Thus, according to Schweitzer, Jesus sent out the twelve on a lightning preaching tour to warn others, not expecting that they would return before the End (cf. Matt. 10:23). However, events did not bear out Jesus' expectations: the disciples did return with no sign of the End coming. So Jesus decided to go to Jerusalem in order to take upon himself the "messianic woes", which were the necessary prelude to the coming of the new age, and thus force the arrival of the Kingdom.

Schweitzer's theories, which make Jesus into something of a disappointed apocalyptic fanatic, will not be repeated here in detail. What should be observed, however, is that Schweitzer's own reconstruction of the life of Jesus was based on precisely the same methodological presuppositions as those of the older nineteenth-century critics. For Schweitzer too had a basic trust in the chronology of the Gospels: Mark's historical sequence, if suitably expanded by the Matthean discourses, was basically accurate and could be used to reconstruct the course of Jesus' ministry. His objection to the older critics was merely that their reconstructions were bad ones, failing to give due weight to the importance of eschatology in Jesus' life and work. His criticisms did nothing to suggest that the whole enterprise of producing a developmental life of Jesus was inherently impossible. Such a claim is implied by Wrede's book, and it is this which makes his work so important.[9]

One of Wrede's concerns was the question of whether Jesus saw himself as Messiah (1971, 1), but it was not this that formed the starting point, or even the major part, of his discussion. Rather, Wrede started with the Gospel of Mark, and with the way in which it had been used by nineteenth-century critics to produce a "life of Jesus". Wrede said that one's primary aim must be to find the meaning and intention of Mark himself, before jumping too hastily to conclusions about the underlying history (1971, 5f).[10] Wrede, like Schweitzer, pointed out how much had to be read into Mark's account before it could yield any neat developmental story. The theory that Jesus wanted to purify Jewish ideas of messiahship is nowhere hinted at in Mark (1971, 15). The secrecy commands fail to fit any scheme of either a gradual growth in understanding by the disciples, or a gradual revelation by Jesus: the theory that Jesus kept his identity secret initially founders on Jesus' explicit claim to be the Son of Man at the start of his ministry (1971, 18; cf. Mark 2:10,28);[11] the confession at Caesarea Philippi can scarcely be the result of a steady growth in understanding by the disciples, since immediately prior to this they are still as blind as ever (8:15ff) and afterwards they remain equally blind (1971, 16). Any idea that Caesarea Philippi formed a great turning-point in Jesus' ministry, with Jesus then starting to teach the disciples about the necessity of the passion, founders on what Wrede saw as a clear prediction of the passion already in the bridegroom saying (2:19f), so that the passion predictions (8:31; 9:31; 10:33) cannot be seen as introducing any new teaching (1971, 21). Wrede thus rejected the old developmental view of the life of Jesus as having no real support in Mark's Gospel. Rather, Mark's whole presentation was dominated by the idea of secrecy, and this could not be satisfactorily explained away by any theory of a growth in understanding, or a steady process of revelation.

Wrede proceeded to analyse the various elements in Mark which, he claimed, were associated with the secrecy motif, and in this he included a very large number of features from Mark. There were Jesus' explicit commands to silence addressed to the demons (1:25,34; 3:12), to those who had witnessed the miracles (1:43f; 5:43; 7:36; 8:26) and to the disciples (8:30; 9:9); Wrede also included instances where Jesus tried to keep his whereabouts a secret (7:24; 9:30f) as well as the attempt by others to silence Bartimaeus (10:47f) (1971, 34ff). These injunctions to silence had been analysed individually by earlier critics, and different explanations for each had been suggested: Jesus might have banned the demons from speaking because they were not on the side of God; Jesus did not wish to have a reputation as a miracle worker; Jesus wanted to avoid false ideas of messiahship, etc.[12] For Wrede these were all unsatisfactory, primarily because such individual explanations could at best only deal with part of the evidence, and the stereotyped form of this feature in Mark suggested that the evidence should all be explained in the same way (1971, 37). Wrede then examined the secrecy charges in great detail, and argued that they were all unhistorical. For example, the injunction to silence after the raising of a girl assumed to be dead (5:43) could not possibly be taken seriously (1971, 50f). Thus he claimed that all these commands were later additions to the tradition.

Wrede also included with the secrecy charges the feature which he called "cryptic speech": e.g., there are instances in Mark where Jesus gives private instruction to only a few people, and some miracles are performed with only a chosen few watching (1971, 53ff, cf. Mark 1:29ff,35; 5:40; 7:17; 10:10). In these cases Wrede was undecided about the question of historicity. However, a clearer case seems to be provided by the so-called "theory of parables", by which Mark's account appears to make Jesus teach in parables in order deliberately to hide his meaning from the crowds (1971, 56ff, cf. Mark 4:10–13; 4:33f). Here Wrede claimed that this could not possibly be historical, since Jesus had never used parables to obscure his message but only to illuminate it (1971, 62, appealing to the work of Jülicher on the parables). Further, since this feature of Mark was to be taken with the other secrecy charges where the issue was Jesus' identity as Messiah, Wrede felt justified in interpreting the "mystery" of 4:11 in the same way: the "mystery" which is withheld from the outside world is the recognition of Jesus' messiahship (1971, 60).

Wrede found the key to all these secrecy passages in the command after the transfiguration, ordering the three disciples to remain silent about what they had seen until after the resurrection (9:9). Wrede claimed that this time limit was intended to apply to *all* the secrecy charges:

> During his earthly life Jesus' messiahship is absolutely a secret and is supposed to be such; no one apart from the confidants of Jesus is supposed to learn about it; with the resurrection, however, its disclosure ensues. This is in fact the crucial idea, the underlying point of Mark's entire approach (1971, 68).

Wrede applied the same explanation to the theory of the use of parables too: the veiling of their meaning was only temporary, and this in turn suggested the true interpretation of 4:21f, which Wrede took as a reference to the revelation of the true meaning of the parables "*after the resurrection*" (1971, 71, Wrede's italics).

Wrede claimed that another theme closely related to the explicit injunctions to silence and the statement about the purpose of parables was the motif of the failure of the disciples to understand Jesus. Here again Wrede rejected the old view that Jesus had tried to teach his disciples gradually. The passion predictions, he claimed, were all unhistorical, since their detailed prophecies, corresponding so precisely to subsequent events, looked like later Christian creations; in any case the fact that the disciples seemed to have been totally unprepared for Jesus' death implied that they had not received any prior instruction (1971, 82ff). There was no evidence of any progression in understanding by the disciples, since they remained totally uncomprehending throughout Jesus' ministry.[13] Further, the motif as it appeared in Mark depended on Mark's literary composition (cf. 8:17, referring to the literary details of the feeding miracles) and hence could not be historical (1971, 104f).

Thus Wrede's conclusion was that all the various aspects of the secrecy theory in Mark were unhistorical. All the secrecy elements in Mark were later additions to the tradition, and reflected the view that "real knowledge of what Jesus is only begins with his resurrection" (1971, 114).

Wrede also considered various elements in Mark which appeared to contradict the secrecy theme: e.g. the parable of the wicked husbandmen *is* understood (12:12), and sometimes Jesus' commands for silence are disobeyed (1:45; 7:36f). However, Wrede claimed that these were no real problem for his theory. Jesus' life story must have been considered worth telling, and hence the veil of secrecy could not have been drawn totally over it. Thus, to a certain extent, it was inevitable that concealment and revelation should coexist (1971, 124ff).

As far as the origin of the secrecy motifs was concerned, Wrede stated quite categorically that these were not due to Mark himself (1971, 145).[14] The various motifs in Mark were too variegated in nature to be the work of a single individual (1971, 145).[15] Although Mark may have agreed with the ideas, they must have originated in the larger circles which influenced him.

After considering the secrecy motifs as they appear in the other three Gospels, Wrede offered an explanation for the origin of the secret in Mark. He suggested that the clue to the whole phenomenon was to be found in what he thought was a very primitive Christian belief that Jesus only became Messiah at the resurrection (1971, 215ff, referring to Acts 2:36; Rom. 1:4; Phil. 2:6ff). However, subsequent Christian reflection led to the rise of the belief that Jesus' earthly life had also been messianic. Wrede therefore suggested that the secrecy motifs were the result of the coming together of these two views, so that Jesus' life was now described as messianic, but with the proviso that this could only be made public after the resurrection.

> It (the secret) can be characterised as the after-effect of the view that the resurrection is the beginning of the messiahship at a time when the life of Jesus was already being filled materially with messianic content. (1971, 229)

Similarly, Mark's picture of the disciples' failure to understand Jesus was a reflection of the revolution in their thinking which the appearances of the risen Jesus caused in them.

One corollary which Wrede drew from his historical explanation of the secret was that, if his theory was correct, then the secret could only have arisen at a time when no explicit messianic claims by Jesus were known. Thus Wrede claimed that his analysis gave "a positive historical testimony for the idea that Jesus actually did not give himself out as messiah" (1971, 230).

Wrede's book has been significant out of all proportion to its size. Whether one agrees with his detailed theories or not, he opened the way to seeing the Gospels as reflecting the beliefs of the early Church, quite as much as reflecting the historical career of Jesus. Nevertheless, his work was by no means universally accepted. Perhaps the most controversial aspect of his total theory was his assertion that Jesus had made no messianic claims, and many thought that Wrede's thesis could be refuted, at least in part, by pointing to messianic elements embedded in the tradition.[16] Such a criticism does not really deal with Wrede's case. His theory was primarily an analysis of *Mark's* Gospel, seeking to show that the secrecy elements were secondary intrusions into the story. His conclusions about the lack of any messianic claim by Jesus was only a corollary tentatively drawn from his attempt to explain the origin of the secrecy motifs. Showing this corollary to be false might show that Wrede's historical explanation was mistaken; but that does not, and cannot, of itself discredit his analysis of Mark's Gospel.[17]

One of Wrede's earliest critics was Schweitzer, who included a discussion of Wrede's book at the end of his *Quest of the Historical Jesus* (328ff). Schweitzer had already published his own theories about the life of Jesus (Schweitzer, 1925), and in his later work he saw no reason to revise his opinions, and indeed he took the opportunity to compare and contrast his own views with those of Wrede. Schweitzer agreed with Wrede in rejecting the psychologizing approach of the nineteenth-century critics. He agreed that the text should be taken as it stood. He agreed too that Mark's text appeared to be full of conflicting elements, which he described as reflecting two basic ideas, one natural and one dogmatic (1954, 335). Further, the secrecy motif was an integral part of the dogmatic element in the tradition. However, at this point, Schweitzer and Wrede parted company. For Wrede, the "dogmatic" element was all unhistorical, and Schweitzer described this view as "thorough-going scepticism". For Schweitzer himself, the dogmatic element was historical and to be explained from the eschatological outlook which dominated Jesus' life and work. Schweitzer labelled his solution "thorough-going eschatology", and claimed that his and Wrede's views were the only possible ones: "tertium non datur" (1954, 335).

Schweitzer criticized Wrede by referring to various features in the life of Jesus which were messianic, e.g. the triumphal entry and the confession before the high priest (1954, 339). Further, he pointed to the difficulty of explaining how the resurrection itself could have given rise to the belief that Jesus was the Messiah: claims that John the Baptist had been raised did not necessarily carry with them any claim that he was the Messiah (1954, 343). Thus Schweitzer looked for the origin of the secrecy charges in Jesus' own life. He claimed that Jesus knew himself to be the Messiah, but that his messiahship was understood in wholly futurist terms. Jesus thus had to keep his identity hidden since his messiahship would only be fully realized in the future when the Kingdom of God came (1925, 185ff). Jesus spoke of his future role as that of the "Son of Man", referring to the time when the Messiah would come as Judge (1925, 191). For others, Jesus and the Son of Man were two different people;

the fact that they were the same was what constituted Jesus' secret (1925, 191f). It was this secret which Peter unwittingly stumbled on at Caesarea Philippi as a result of what he had seen at the transfiguration (Schweitzer was forced to rearrange the Marcan chronology at this point [1925, 174ff; 1954, 380ff]). Thus before the secret could be divulged too widely, Jesus had to go to Jerusalem to force the arrival of the Kingdom by himself undergoing the messianic woes. Jesus was betrayed to the authorities by Judas, the content of what Judas betrayed being the secret itself: Judas told the Jewish leaders that Jesus had identified himself as the coming Messiah (1925, 216f). Thus Jesus was condemned to death for the blasphemy of claiming to be Messiah.

The weaknesses of Schweitzer's position are clear today. His reliance on the synoptic chronology has been vitiated by the work of the form critics. Further, Schweitzer can scarcely be said to have been true to his own avowed principles of taking the text as it stands and not reading between the lines (cf. his rearrangement of the transfiguration story, or his claim to know what it was that Judas betrayed). So too form criticism has shown that the early Church did adapt the tradition as it was handed on in a way which Schweitzer rejected almost *a priori* (1954, 338).

Nevertheless, if Schweitzer's total theory has found little support, several details of his arguments against Wrede have been used by others. Among these is the argument that the resurrection is insufficient in itself to explain the rise of the belief that Jesus was the Messiah.[18] In Germany several of the early critics of Wrede agreed with Schweitzer in seeing the origin of the secrecy motifs in the life of Jesus, even if some were prepared to admit that the secrecy theory might have been secondarily expanded in the tradition. For example, J. Weiss and Wernle both conceded that some of the secrecy elements were secondary,[19] but claimed that the basic idea could be traced back to Jesus' own ministry. Wernle claimed that some of the secrecy charges were due to Jesus' desire to preach about God and the things of God, rather than about himself (1917, 334). For Weiss, some of the secrecy charges were intelligible in the life of Jesus and reflected the belief, common to Jesus and the earliest Church, that Jesus' messiahship was futurist, i.e. Jesus would become Messiah at a future date (for the earliest Church this was the resurrection) (1903, 45ff). Thus not all the secrecy charges in the tradition were unhistorical. In particular, Weiss claimed that the command to silence in 1:25 was probably historical, even though he conceded that the general statements in 1:34 and 3:11f might be secondary (1903, 53,146f).[20]

Weiss also claimed that the command to silence after Peter's confession (8:30) was historical, and he adopted the traditional theory that Jesus was here seeking to avoid political ideas popularly associated with messiahship.[21]

In England, opposition to Wrede was far more unequivocal in asserting that the secrecy elements in the tradition stemmed from Jesus. Schweitzer's results, which affirmed the historicity of the gospel narratives, were generally found to be more acceptable than the radical scepticism about the question of historicity which Wrede's results seemed to offer.[22] The most influential attack was that of Sanday (1907, 70–6). Sanday's language was intemperate,[23] but effective: indeed one modern writer could even say that "Sanday said all that really needs to be said about Wrede".[24] However, Sanday's only real argument of substance was the argument of the inadequacy of the resurrection to explain the rise of the belief that Jesus was the Messiah. Sanday's own explanation of the secrecy elements in the Gospels changed over the years. In an article in 1904, he adopted the traditional view that Jesus was modifying the popular idea of messiahship, from one involving military warfare to one of suffering service.[25] In his later lectures of 1907, Sanday inclined more to Schweitzer's idea of Jesus' messiahship being partly futurist: the secrecy charges reflected Jesus' reserve about making messianic claims, since "although He was the Messiah, the time for entering upon His full Messianic functions was not yet" (1907, 119). And this idea that messiahship involves a future role, or at least an as yet uncompleted task, has been supported by others since Sanday as explaining Jesus' reserve about himself.[26]

By far the most common explanation of at least part of the secrecy complex in Mark amongst those who would trace its origin back to Jesus himself has been the traditional view that Jesus wished to reinterpret the popular idea of messiahship, and to avoid any political overtones inherent in the title.[27] Such a theory runs into difficulties as a comprehensive treatment of Wrede's case. It involves a certain amount of reading between the lines: Mark himself gives no suggestion explicitly that the title "Messiah" needed modification before being acceptable to Jesus. Wrede himself had already pointed out that a more natural way for Jesus to have proceeded would have been to have given some explicit teaching on the subject rather than simply enjoining silence.[28] Further, such an explanation can only apply to some of the texts considered by Wrede. It *might* be appropriate in explaining the secrecy charge at 8:30,[29] but not in explaining other passages, e.g. the commands to silence after miracles. Thus many who adopt this type of explanation for 8:30 have to give different explanations for other secrecy texts.[30]

Others have seen the secret in more comprehensive terms within the life of Jesus. For Schniewind, the secret was not something confined to single verses: rather, it underlay every synoptic pericope (1963, 56; cf. Taylor, 1954). Schniewind explicitly took up the ideas of Bultmann who had presented the picture of Jesus as the prophet of the End-time whose message signified the presence of the eschatological time of salvation (Bultmann, 1951, 3–32). For Bultmann this implicitly involved a Christology.[31] Schniewind turned this round and identified this implicit Christology with the messianic secret. Thus the secret consisted of the fact that eschatology had now become joyfully present in Jesus' own proclamation, in his call to repentance and in his offer of forgiveness (1952, 6). Yet the one who brings the offer of the presence of the Kingdom is the non-royal Messiah coming with the powerless word. "The secret of the reign of God is the secret of the word" (1952, 10). Nevertheless, despite the force of much of what is said about Jesus here, this does not really tackle the question of why the secrecy motifs appear in the way they do in *Mark*, apparently often in editorial, rather than traditional, passages.[32]

Not unrelated to Schniewind's approach was that of Lohmeyer, who also saw the secret as underlying the whole tradition. He too traced the idea back to Jesus himself, but admitted that Mark had developed the idea considerably.[33] For Lohmeyer, Jesus was both an ordinary man among men, and also the Son of Man, the eschatological bringer of salvation. The messianic secret is the result of the juxtaposition of these two radically different roles in the person of Jesus. In Jesus, the Son of Man has become man and hence there is an inherent duality in Jesus of hidden and revealed, exalted and lowly, divine and human. Any such duality in the tradition led Lohmeyer to interpret the text in terms of a Son of Man Christology.[34] But as Son of Man, Jesus is still essentially part of the divine realm rather than the human, and as such he is opposed by this world and finally rejected.[35] Thus Lohmeyer reinterpreted the "messianic" secret as a "Son of Man" secret. However, he never really developed his theories about how the secret was seen by Mark. Further, there was a basic assumption in his work that when what is eschatological, or other-worldly, enters human history, it must take the form of a *hidden* reality (cf. Sjöberg, 1955, 122f) and this is by no means easy to maintain in the light of Jewish apocalyptic ideas in general.

At this point the work of Sjöberg becomes important. Sjöberg, like Lohmeyer, sought to find the roots of the secrecy motifs in the Son of Man title, but he went further in trying to show why Jesus as Son of Man must be a hidden figure. Like Lohmeyer, Sjöberg conceded that Mark might have developed some of the secrecy elements in the tradition, but the fundamental idea went back to Jesus himself and to the ideas associated with the title Son of Man which he adopted (246). Sjöberg claimed that the idea of hiddenness was inherent in Jewish apocalyptic beliefs about the Son of Man–Messiah. He referred to the idea, found in some later rabbis, of the Messiah living on earth, hidden and unrecognized (72–80). Although the evidence for this was late (post-Christian), Sjöberg claimed that these examples showed how the concept of a hidden Messiah could arise within Judaism (82). A closer parallel to the gospel accounts was to be found in the apocalyptic figure of the Son of Man. The Jewish evidence, especially 1 Enoch and 4 Ezra, showed a basic idea of the Son of Man as a heavenly being who would remain hidden until revealed to all at the eschaton (48f). There was too the general belief that, although apocalyptic secrets would be fully revealed at the end of time, God had already revealed these secrets to a chosen few (1ff). This then was the background for the secrecy elements in the Gospels: Jesus on earth was the Son of Man, but he was only revealed as such to a chosen few, whilst from the rest of the world he must remain hidden.

Sjöberg's theories have not gone uncriticized.[36] The idea of a hidden Messiah on earth is not attested prior to the 2nd century A.D.[37] The dates of 1 Enoch and 4 Ezra may also provide a problem if these writings are to be used as evidence of pre-Christian ideas.[38] But in any case, the Son of Man in 1 Enoch and 4 Ezra differs significantly from the Gospels' presentation in that in the former the Son of Man remains inactive in heaven, whereas in the latter Jesus is active on earth.[39] There is thus no real parallel to the idea of a Son of Man, or Messiah, hidden but active on earth prior to the eschaton. Moreover, the secrecy charges in Mark are, almost without exception, quite separate from references to Jesus as Son of Man; rather the two strands in Mark, i.e. secrecy and Son of Man, seem unrelated.

This then is a brief survey of some of the attempts to deal with Wrede's case by locating the origin of the secrecy elements in Mark's Gospel in the ministry of Jesus himself. The most forceful modern presentation of the view that the secret is basically historical is the article of Dunn reprinted here, where Dunn seeks to give a broader justification for the theory that Jesus was seeking to modify traditional ideas of messiahship, by referring to a wider selection of texts than just the secrecy charges themselves. However, in all these attempts to deal with the messianic secret, it still remains questionable whether Wrede's case has been met on its own terms, viz. as an analysis of *Mark*. How do the secrecy elements function for Mark, and why do the secrecy charges appear in the redactional strand of the Gospel?[40] E.g., Dunn allows the possibility of a redactional secrecy motif in 1:34 and 3:11f, but he does not develop this further.[41] The significance which Mark saw in the secret still therefore requires an explanation.[42]

Wrede's book has always been more favourable received in Germany than in England. In England, discussion has often centred on the question of historicity, and many have been content to trace the secrecy elements back to Jesus himself. In Germany, since the rise of form criticism, there has always been a greater willingness to accept some, if not all, of Wrede's evidence as indicating the existence of secondary elements in the tradition. In particular, the form critics Bultmann and Dibelius accepted much of Wrede's theory, even though some of the details were changed significantly.

Bultmann adopted Wrede's theory enthusiastically. Indeed he believed that the theory proved quite conclusively that Jesus had never claimed to be Messiah. (See especially his 1919 article.) Although always claiming to be adopting Wrede's results *in toto*, Bultmann made one significant alteration in that he assumed that the secrecy theory was due to Mark himself, whereas Wrede had claimed that it was pre-Marcan.[43] Many have agreed with this alteration to Wrede's original theory. However, this then creates difficulties for Wrede's explanation about the origin of the secret, as stemming from the juxtaposition of a non-messianic and a messianic view of Jesus' earthly life. For Mark himself seems unaware of a non-messianic view, and hence Wrede's historical explanation requires modification.[44] However the need for such a modification was not recognized by Bultmann himself. Bultmann endorsed Dibelius' description of Mark's Gospel as a "book of secret epiphanies", and he characterized Mark as "the union of the Hellenistic kerygma about Christ ... with the tradition of the story of Jesus" (1963, 347f). This assertion by Bultmann, if taken very broadly, has been extremely influential, as we shall see.

Dibelius too endorsed Wrede's theory in some respects, although he also made some modifications. He claimed that the number of features which Wrede had included from Mark should be reduced.

E.g., the withdrawal of Jesus from the crowds to perform miracles (cf. 5:40; 7:33; 8:23) is nothing to do with the messianic secret but is simply a standard feature in such miracle stories (Dibelius, 93f); on the other hand, the injunctions to silence after the miracles *are* part of Mark's messianic secret (73f).[45] Like Bultmann, Dibelius ascribed the secrecy theory to Mark's own redaction, but he interpreted it differently. For Dibelius, its origin lay in Mark's concern to explain the fact that Jesus' messiahship had not been universally recognized. Mark used the secret to show

> why He was not recognized as Messiah by the people and why He was opposed, despised, and finally sent to the cross. In this way the gospel of Mark was written as *a book of secret epiphanies* (230).

This is one of the classic presentations of the so-called "apologetic" explanation of the secret, i.e. seeing it as a device to explain to later readers Jesus' conspicuous lack of success. It is a type of explanation which has always had considerable support, and is represented in this volume by the contribution of T. A. Burkill.[46]

However, as an explanation of all the secrecy elements in Mark as assembled by Wrede, the apologetic theory is not entirely satisfactory. Wrede himself said that he considered the theory at first, but rejected it on the grounds that Mark's presentation of the secret "at no point awakens the impression that in this we are dealing with an apologetic evasion" (1971, 226).[47] Above all the apologetic theory fails to account for the element of revelation which exists alongside the element of secrecy in Mark. The commands to silence are sometimes broken (1:45, 7:36f); and Jesus' condemnation to death in Mark is not the result of any secrecy being imposed: on the contrary, it is precisely due to the veil of secrecy being lifted (14:61f). Thus Jesus' lack of success cannot be due simply to lack of knowledge on the part of the crowds and the Jewish authorities arising from the secrecy charges: for Mark's own presentation shows that such knowledge *was* at times available to others. The apologetic theory can provide a good explanation for the saying about the purpose of parables in 4:11f, but the conjunction of messianic revelation with messianic secrecy is more difficult.[48]

If then the breaking of the secret causes difficulty for the apologetic theory, it was precisely this which formed the basis for the interpretation of H. J. Ebeling, in what is sometimes called the "epiphanic" interpretation of the secret. Ebeling claimed that Mark's Gospel is to be understood as primarily kerygmatic, i.e. as an expression of the kerygma in Mark's day. Attempts to use the Gospel to discover anything about the underlying history of Jesus' own ministry are simply inappropriate to the nature of the gospel material. The messianic secret must therefore also be interpreted in terms of the kerygma. As far as Mark was concerned, there was no question but that Jesus' life was seen as messianic, as the epiphany of the Son of God. Hence there was no possibility that any of the secrecy elements could be trying to hide this fact. Thus these elements were all interpreted by Ebeling as literary devices which simply highlight the glory of Jesus and stress the epiphanic nature of the events concerned. So, for example, the main point in the commands to silence is not the commands themselves; rather the stress is on the way in which such commands are repeatedly broken, and the commands simply highlight the irresistible way in which Jesus' fame spread (115ff). Similarly, the failure of the disciples to understand Jesus' teaching is merely a stylistic device which conveys to the reader the idea of the transcendent nature of the revelation being given (146ff). The Marcan theory about parables serves a similar aim: the characters in the text differ, in that the disciples are distinguished from the outside world which does not understand; nevertheless, the basic idea remains the same: the readers are shown that they too belong within the circle of those to whom the mystery has been revealed, and this implies both their privileged position as well as the responsibilities entailed (179ff).

Ebeling's interpretation brought into prominence Mark's own kerygmatic purpose; so too it took seriously the element of revelation which exists alongside the element of secrecy. Nevertheless, his theory has won little support as the means of explaining all the secrecy elements in Mark,[49] though some have adopted this type of explanation for part of the evidence.[50] Ebeling's approach was undoubtedly very one-sided in driving a deep wedge between kerygma and history, as if the latter had no place in discussing the former. If Mark was so interested in the present kerygma, *and* so uninterested in past history, it is strange that he should have chosen to dress up his version of the kerygma in a form which appears to be a description of past history.[51] Further, the theory runs into some difficulties within the Gospel itself. The key to Ebeling's interpretation was the fact that some commands to silence are disobeyed. But this does not cover all the secrecy charges, since at times there is no mention of their being broken. Ebeling was thus sometimes forced to read an implied breaking of the command into the Marcan text. E.g. the order in 5:43 was seen by Ebeling as so clearly historically impossible that the reader *must* have assumed that it could not be obeyed.[52]

But the text itself gives no justification for this. The time limit in 9:9 also causes difficulties for Ebeling, as Strecker points out.[53] The apocalyptic idea which Ebeling referred to, of a secret to be universally revealed at a future date, does not provide a true parallel to the text of Mark here: in other apocalyptic literature the time of revelation is future, whereas in Mark the time in question is now past.

The tension in Mark between secrecy and revelation thus causes difficulty for both the apologetic and epiphanic interpretations of the secret. In Wrede's theory, this tension was closely connected with the temporal distinction: the period before the resurrection is the time of secrecy, but after Easter a new situation arises. The significance of the resurrection as marking the boundary line between secrecy and revelation has also been stressed by Percy (286ff). Like Wrede, Percy claimed that the secret was due to the coming together of two streams of the tradition. However, he disagreed with Wrede's claim that one of these streams had viewed Jesus' life as unmessianic, for the secret in Mark was not just an auxiliary concept and appeared to be more far-reaching than Wrede's theory implied (280). So Percy suggested that the secret was the result of one stream of tradition, which had always viewed Jesus' life as messianic, being met by another which had reflected more deeply on the importance of the cross and resurrection. Thus Percy claimed that Mark's Gospel is to be interpreted as very similar to the Pauline kerygma (cf. 1 Cor. 2:8; 2 Cor. 13:4; Phil. 2:7f), where Jesus' earthly life is to be seen as one of humility and lowliness, and his true glory only dates from the resurrection. In Mark, "lowliness" is replaced by "secrecy", but the basic idea remains the same.[54] Thus the disciples *could* not see Jesus' true glory prior to Easter, and given this understanding of the importance of the cross, the secrecy charges and the general failure to understand Jesus during his earthly life appear as a necessary part of the story.[55] The time limit set to the period of secrecy in 9:9 is thus taken very seriously. The period of secrecy is Jesus' earthly life and is now past. A very similar view is represented in this collection of essays by the article of G. Strecker.

Nevertheless, it is not clear that this view can solve all the problems of the secret. There are difficulties raised by those points in Mark where the secret is broken *prior* to Easter (cf. 1:45; 7:36).[56] Further, if it is true that the secret belongs primarily to the past, then it is not clear why Mark should have taken the trouble to stress it so much in his Gospel, and it becomes doubtful whether it has kerygmatic significance.[57]

This interpretation has clear links with Bultmann's claim that

Mark is setting the stories about Jesus in terms of the (hellenistic) kerygma. Others have tried to develop Bultmann's insight along different lines. One extreme example of this has been the comprehensive interpretation of Mark's Gospel by J. Schreiber in terms of a gnostic redeemer myth. Applied to the secrecy elements in Mark, Jesus' hiddenness and his failure to be understood are compared to the ideas in the gnostic myth where the redeemer is unrecognized by the supernatural powers (cf. 1 Cor. 2:8) (Schreiber, 156f). However, this theory has been heavily criticized. Without going into the vexed question of whether there was a pre-Christian redeemer myth, Mark's Gospel lacks vital elements in the proposed scheme: there is no idea of pre-existence in Mark, nor is there any typically gnostic cosmology reflected in Mark; further, the distinctive feature of Mark is that Jesus *is* recognized by the supernatural powers but not by men.[58]

If the attempt to interpret Mark in gnostic terms has found little support, Bultmann's thesis has been fruitful in a slightly different direction. Probably the most decisive contribution has been that of H. Conzelmann. Conzelmann accepts Wrede's analysis of the secrecy texts as indicating that they are secondary additions to the tradition. However, he rejects Wrede's explanation of their origin, referring to what has become the standard critique of Wrede's original theory, viz., that Mark's material was never understood non-messianically (1968, 42). Conzelmann ascribes the secret to Mark, and says:

> His contribution does not consist in his forcing non-messianic elements into a framework of christological belief, but rather in his putting together a mass of materials already understood christologically in such a way as to conform to the kerygma (understood in the sense of the secrecy christology) (1968, 42).

He says that, "It is not the non-messianic character of the units in the tradition which causes the evangelist trouble, but rather their messianic character", so that the secret represents "an expression of a positive understanding of revelation" (1968, 42f). The secret is thus the means whereby Mark *controls* the Christology of his tradition by pointing to the cross (cf. 1970, 181f). Only by such a means can Mark prevent his account from becoming a series of unambiguous epiphanies of a divine being,[59] or, in Conzelmann's famous words, "the secrecy theory is the hermeneutical presupposition of the genre 'gospel'" (1968, 43).

Clearly Conzelmann's interpretation has much in common with the theory of Percy and Strecker: both stress the centrality of the cross for

Mark as the determining factor in any interpretation of the life of Jesus; so too, both claim that a true understanding of Jesus is only possible after the resurrection. Nevertheless, there is an important difference: for Strecker and others, the secret is a matter of past history alone; for Conzelmann the secret still applies in the present:

> The faithful – i.e. the readers of the book – are shown the mystery in such a way that it remains veiled from the world even after Easter. It can only be grasped through faith, i.e. in the church. To those without it remains hidden (1969, 139).[60]

This theory, that the secret reflects the central importance of the cross as the only valid key for interpreting the person of Jesus, has found widespread support.[61] It is represented in this volume by the article of E. Schweizer, who also stresses the importance of discipleship, of "following" Jesus in the way of the cross. This pastoral aspect of the secret is also brought out by others: the disciple too must follow in the same way of humility and service as his master.[62] Thus, according to this interpretation, the secret is Mark's way of developing his *theologia crucis*. The cross and resurrection are thus the "ending" of the secret in that they provide the key to the interpretation of the whole, and indeed the story itself is told in such a way as to lead up to this ending.[63]

One very popular further development of this theory has been the attempt to specify in more detail the Christology which Mark is seeking to control by the secret. Many have seen Mark as deliberately opposing a specific Christology in his community, usually described as a *theios anēr* Christology, i.e. a view which sees Jesus primarily in terms of a great miracle worker and the possessor of supernatural power.[64] In this respect reference is often made to D. Georgi's study on Paul's opponents in 2 Corinthians. Many would claim that there is a close link between the Christology of Paul's opponents and the Christology which Mark is seeking to control: both profess a *theios anēr* type of Christology and couple this with a belief that the same miraculous powers have been handed on to the community. The most thorough-going interpretation of Mark's Gospel along these lines is that of Weeden, who sees Mark's attitude as one of outright opposition to such a Christology. Others, such as Luz, would see Mark as trying to correct the views of his community rather more gently, by incorporation rather than by outright opposition.[65] In either case Mark is seen as taking the stress away from the miracles and pointing to the cross as the decisive event for reaching a true evaluation of Jesus.[66]

Overall, the theory that the secret is Mark's way of stressing the centrality of the cross is very attractive. It takes seriously the results of form criticism which sees that a non-messianic Jesus tradition is hard to envisage; it also takes seriously the time limit set in 9:9 (even if it has to interpret this as referring to only the possibility of understanding after Easter); above all it seeks to explain the relationship between history and kerygma which is involved in the writing of any "Gospel".[67] Nevertheless, there are still problems. Why do some of the miracle stories lack a secrecy charge (e.g. 5:1–20)?[68] Why too are some of the secrecy charges disobeyed whilst others are not?

These are the main lines of interpretation of the messianic secret in Mark. Many have followed Wrede in assuming that the texts which he collected are all to be explained in the same way. This has frequently been contested by those who would see the secrecy elements as originating in Jesus' own ministry.[69] However, even amongst those who would see Marcan redaction at work in some parts of the secrecy material, there is one part of Wrede's evidence which is often discussed separately from the rest. This is the motif of the disciples' lack of understanding. Many would claim that this should be considered separately from the other secrecy passages. For example, Tyson points out that, in the rest of the secrecy material, people recognize Jesus' true identity but are forbidden to publicize it, whereas the disciples have a wrong conception of Jesus' nature.[70]

Very diverse positions have been adopted with regard to this apparently unfavourable portrait of the disciples in Mark. One view which has attracted a lot of interest is that the disciples represent a group within Mark's own community, and Mark's unfavourable picture represents a polemical attitude towards this group. This view is represented in this volume by the article of Tyson, who claims that the disciples represent the Jerusalem church of Mark's day: these Christians have too narrow a view of messiahship (conceiving of it solely in royal terms), and fail to give central importance to the cross. The view that the Jerusalem church is under attack in Mark is also shared by others.[71] By far the most thorough-going explanation of Mark along these lines is that of T. J. Weeden. Weeden does not specify the geographical location of Mark's opponents, but he sees them as represented by the disciples in the Gospel, and, like Tyson, he sees them as having an erroneous Christology. Peter's confession at 8:29 shows that he only understands Jesus as the Christ on the basis of the miracles: it is thus the confession of Jesus as a *theios anēr*. Weeden believes that the opponents based their claims on resurrection appearances which gave them positions of privilege and power. By contrast, he claims, Mark writes his story in such a way as to deny any resurrection appearances to the opponents at all: the transfiguration, claimed by the opponents to be a resurrection appearance, is put back into the ministry of Jesus, and the secrecy charge of 9:9 shows how such a claim by the opponents might arise (news of the story only originated after Easter) but also that it is false. The silence of the women at the tomb (16:8) shows that the disciples never received the angels' message and so can never have seen the risen Jesus.[72]

Such a reading of Mark is not without its difficulties. This wholly negative view of the disciples had already been rejected by Wrede,[73] and it involves a certain amount of forcing of the evidence. The ending of Mark (cf. 16:7) suggests a theophany and hence a restoration of the disciples, rather than their final rejection.[74] Further, negative features about the disciples are balanced by equally positive ones.[75] It is thus by no means clear that the disciples' role is one of implacable doctrinal opposition to Jesus.[76] Thus other critics would see the disciples' role in Mark more positively.[77] Also it may be that not all the passages originally listed by Wrede in this category have the same function: some may be using the motif of lack of understanding simply to highlight the importance of the miracle or teaching in question, and not all the passages suggest that the incomprehension is culpable.[78] Thus although the theory that Mark may be trying to correct another christological view by the secret is widely accepted, the refinement which would identify the disciples with the proponents of such a Christology is more difficult to sustain.

The problem of the unity of the secrecy motifs has also been raised by others, independently of the question of the disciples' incomprehension. We have seen that all the main explanations of the meaning of the secret in Mark explain different parts of the evidence very well, but each has its own difficulties. Thus a feature of some recent discussions of the problem has been the questioning of Wrede's initial premiss that all the secrecy texts must be explained in the same way, and the adoption of different explanations for various parts of the evidence. The most influential attempt to do this is that of U. Luz, who distinguishes two distinct motifs in Mark. The commands to silence after miracles are to be interpreted in the light of their being broken, and hence they simply highlight Jesus' glory as a miracle-worker (i.e. an "epiphanic" interpretation for this part of the evidence); however, the commands to silence which concern Jesus' identity (1:34; 3:11f; 8:30) are *not* disobeyed, and these show that Jesus' true identity can only be understood in the light of the cross.[79]

There has been a tendency among others to discount Mark's theological contribution almost entirely. For Trocmé, Wrede's collection of texts is really only a hotch-potch of unrelated material. He claims that the secrecy charges after miracles are the exception rather than the rule and are probably pre-Marcan; the commands to the demons are simply a suppression of praise from those who cannot be disciples; the failure of the disciples to understand has nothing to do with a *messianic* secret; the private instruction given to the disciples is never christological, but simply serves as a literary device to highlight the particular teaching involved. "In other words, under close scrutiny, the theory of the Messianic Secret simply vanishes for lack of evidence" (1973, 10). The most recent full-length discussion of the problem is that of H. Räisänen, whose concluding chapter is reproduced in this volume. Räisänen too questions the unity of the secrecy motifs. Different explanations probably apply in different cases. The "real" messianic secret only includes the commands to silence about Jesus' identity (1:34; 3:11f; 8:30). Räisänen argues that these texts are probably redactional, and he tentatively adopts a solution similar to that of Percy, that Jesus' true identity is only recognizable after Easter. However, he says that one should not exaggerate Mark's own theological contribution: there were many, at times contradictory, elements in the pre-Marcan tradition, and Mark may have been content to hand these on, rather than impose a consistent, theological viewpoint on the material. A similar view is taken by R. Pesch in his recent commentary on Mark. Pesch quotes Räisänen's conclusions extensively to show agreement with his own views. However, he goes even further than Räisänen in ascribing 3:11f and 8:30 to the pre-Marcan tradition. Thus only 1:34 is taken to be due to Mark's redaction. Mark is, for Pesch, the "conservative redactor", not the creative theologian which modern redaction critics have suggested.[80]

If the idea of the existence of the messianic secret in Mark is not rejected as a modern invention, there is still the problem of whether the secret should be regarded as an isolated phenomenon within early Christianity. Precise parallels in Judaism are not easy to discover, as we have seen. Wrede himself pointed to a few similar features in the Fourth Gospel, but concluded that "the actual idea of the messianic secret seems to have had only a short history" (1971, 244). This has been questioned in J. M. Robinson's recent article (1978). Parallels for some parts of the secrecy complex in

Mark, viz. the parable theory and the belief that Easter marked the dividing line between secrecy and revelation, are now amply documented from the Nag Hammadi texts. Jesus' mysterious teaching is there interpreted to the chosen few, usually after Easter. Robinson thus questions whether Wrede was right to concentrate primarily on the silencing commands and the question of Jesus' identity. Further, he points to the fact that in 8:32 Jesus speaks "openly", prior to Easter. Thus Robinson argues:

> There seems to be in Mark an effort to push back the hermeneutical turning point from Easter to the point in the so-called public ministry when Jesus began to teach kerygmatically ... It may be that we have to do here with what was in substance the rationale for the *genre* Gospel, as an emergent orthodoxy sought to validate Jesus prior to his death as a source of ultimate interpretation and not just as what emergent Gnosticism could all-too-readily dispense with, a coded text (1978, 142).

This attempt to use the Nag Hammadi texts to illuminate the messianic secret no doubt merits further discussion. Clearly there are problems of dating: how far is it legitimate to use these later gnostic texts as background for the earlier canonical Gospels? With regard to Robinson's specific points, it is possible that Wrede placed too much stress on the silencing commands. But these commands are still part of the secrecy complex in Mark, and it is not clear how they are illuminated by the gnostic texts. Moreover, 9:9, which comes after the "open" teaching in 8:32, still suggests that Easter will mark a significant turning-point in the revelation of what is secret. Nevertheless, Robinson's essay may show where further insights into the significance of the messianic secret may be gained.

This survey shows that there is a wide divergence of opinion about the correct interpretation of the secrecy elements in Mark. Most critics today would probably agree that Wrede's original explanation of the secret is not tenable, and that he tried to explain too many features of Mark's Gospel by his theory. (E.g. the secrecy charge in 1:25, and the privacy motif in the miracles, are probably standard features of such stories.) However, unanimity ends there. The problems of how much in Mark should be considered as part of the "messianic secret", how much goes back to Jesus, whether it is right to explain all the secrecy texts by a single theory, etc., are all questions which continue to receive different answers. There has been a recent trend, especially amongst American scholars, to use the methods and insights of literary criticism in analysing the gospel texts, and it may well be that such an approach may shed further light on the messianic secret in Mark.[81] Insights from the field of sociology may also be fruitful,[82] and the Nag Hammadi texts, now fully available in translated form, may enable us to extend the background against which we can interpret the Gospels.

The problems of the messianic secret in Mark is not of academic interest alone. Some earlier critics of Wrede's book believed that the conclusions which he drew about the lack of any messianic claims by Jesus undermined the basis of Christian faith. Others who have been more prepared to accept this feature of Wrede's theory would see the secret in Mark as the result of later Christians struggling with the problems of their faith in new situations. The latter approach makes the messianic secret no less relevant for contemporary Christianity than the former. For only in dialogue with the past, and with Christians who struggled to respond to their own situation, can Christians today begin to work out what their attitudes should be.

## NOTES

1 Wrede, 1971. The term "messianic secret" has become the conventional English equivalent of the German *Messiasgeheimnis* (the term which Wrede used in the original title of his book in German in 1901) and so has been used here. However the German word *Geheimnis* carries the sense of "mystery" as well as "secret", so that a rigid translation of *Geheimnis* by "secret" is sometimes misleading.

2 The importance of Wrede's work is particularly stressed by Bultmann, 1964, 41f. Cf. also W. C. Robinson, pp. 97f here.

3 Cf. D. R. Catchpole's review of Wrede's book, *EvQ* 46 (1974) 55f.

4 Cf. the comments of W. G. Kümmel, *Introduction to the New Testament* (London: SCM/Nashville and New York: Abingdon, 1975) 91: "The aim of the evangelist in introducing the dogmatic theory is in no way clearly perceptible", and Luz: "The messianic secret is still a mystery" (p. 75 here).

5 Histories of research are to be found in Ebeling, 1939; Percy, 1953, 271ff; Clark, 1962; Blevins, 1965; Glasswell, 1965a; Minette de Tillesse, 1968, 9–34; Aune, 1969, 1–13; Räisänen, 1976, 18–49; Powley, 1979. However, nearly all of these are either not in English, or not easily available to the general reader, being in the form of unpublished theses.

6 H. J. Holtzmann, *Die synoptischen Evangelien* (Leipzig: Engelmann, 1863); B. Weiss, *A Manual of Introduction to the New Testament* (ET London: Hodder & Stoughton, 1888), both building on the earlier studies of C. G. Wilke, *Der Urevangelist* (Leipzig, 1838) and C. H. Weisse, *Die evangelische Geschichte* (Leipzig, 1838).

7 This is of course a non sequitur: the fact that Mark is earlier than the other Gospels can show nothing about its historical reliability in absolute terms.

8 See Wrede's own summary (1971, 11f); also Räisänen, 1976, 19.

9 Thus Wrede is probably more important than Schweitzer in bringing to an end the "old quest" for the historical Jesus: see J. M. Robinson, 1959, 32ff.

10 See, however, Robinson's article here for doubts about how far Wrede was true to his own principles in this respect.

11 Wrede rejected the view that "Son of Man" here might be a roundabout way of saying "I" or "man" by claiming that for *Mark* it must be a messianic designation. (Wrede tended to use the term "messianic" somewhat loosely to refer to anything which suggested that Jesus had supernatural power and authority.)

12 See Wrede's own summary of the views of his predecessors (1971, 255ff).

13 Wrede referred to 4:13; 4:40–1; 6:50–2; 7:18; 8:16–21; 9:5f; 9:19; 10:24; 14:37–41 (1971, 101f).

14 Wrede has frequently been misread as claiming that the secret is due to Mark himself (cf. Räisänen, 24, for a list of authors). But see also Robinson's article here, where he shows how, in most of his book, Wrede appears to assume that the secret is the work of Mark himself, and only introduces the theory of a pre-Marcan stage at the end of his analysis.

15 Robinson says that Wrede appealed to "inconsistencies" (pp. 98f here); however, Wrede only spoke of elements that were unresolved or unharmonized (*unausgeglichenes*), which is perhaps rather weaker than "inconsistent".

16 Cf. Schweitzer's criticism of Wrede, noted below; also Taylor, 1948; Aune, 1969; see too Dunn's essay reprinted here.

17 Cf. the comment of Barbour, 1968, 327: "Much of Wrede's theory about Mark could still be true even if Jesus had as a matter of history only forborne to make Messianic claims because they would be misunderstood."

18 See Jülicher, 1906, 23; Bousset, 1906, 168f (Bousset later changed his mind about the secret: see n. 46 below). In England the same argument was used by Sanday, 1907, 75f; Peake, 1924, 56; Rawlinson, 1925, 260; Taylor, 1948, 147. The argument has some validity, but it is by no means clear that the only alternative is that the title stems from Jesus' own claims for himself during his ministry. Cf. N. A. Dahl, "The Crucified Messiah", in *The Crucified Messiah and Other Essays* (ET Minneapolis: Augsburg, 1974) 10–36, who argues that the title Messiah may derive primarily from the charges made against Jesus at his trial: Jesus' silence in the face of the charge meant that he was crucified as Messiah. The early Church then turned this into a positive confession of faith in the light of the resurrection, seen as God's vindication of the crucified Messiah.

19 See n. 46 below.

20 Wrede replied to Weiss in his later article of 1904, this being virtually the only answer made by Wrede to his critics (he died in 1906). Wrede still defended his thesis by referring to the stereotyped nature of these commands as implying a common origin for them all. (For a similar modern view, see Horstmann, 1969, 125.) In fact Wrede was probably on weak ground here: many would now see the command in 1:25 as traditional in Mark, the silencing of the demon being the standard means whereby the power of the demon is overcome – cf. O. Bauernfeind's programmatic study, *Die Worte der Dämonen im Markusevangelium* (Stuttgart, 1927). See too Bultmann, 1963, 209f; Kee, 1977, 169; and several others including Luz, p. 81 here, and Strecker, p. 51 here.

21 Weiss, 1903, 236f; Bousset, 1906, 172ff; Wernle, 1917, 339.

22 For the generally negative reaction of English scholarship to German "scepticism" in the earlier part of this century, see Robert Morgan, "Non Angli sed Angeli: Some Anglican Reactions to German Gospel Criticism", in S. W. Sykes, D. Holmes (ed.), *New Studies in Theology I* (London: Duckworth, 1980) 1–30. Cf. Peake's comment: "Wrede's solution has met with little or any acceptance. And rightly so, for it involves a scepticism as to the trustworthiness of our narratives so radical that, if it could be justified, we could hardly trust them for anything" (1924, 56). This can scarcely be called a scientific argument!

23 He said that Wrede wrote "in the style of a Prussian official" with "all the arrogance of a certain sort of common sense" (70). He accused Wrede of a lack of imagination (70) and called his theory "utterly artificial and impossible" (74).

24 S. Neill, *The Interpretation of the New Testament 1861–1961* (Oxford: OUP, 1966) 248.

25 The secrecy must be "connected with the recasting of the Messianic idea which our Lord certainly carried out, divesting it of its associations with political action and transforming it from a kingdom of this world to a Kingdom of God and of the Spirit" (1904, 324).

26 Cf. Taylor, 1948, 151: "In truth the Messiah, He would not be the Messiah until His task was accomplished." Cf. too Longenecker, 1969, noting possible parallels with the Teacher of Righteousness at Qumran and Bar Kochbah, claims that "no man can be defined as a messiah in Judaism before he has accomplished the task of the anointed" (213, quoting Flusser). See too Dunn, p. 129 here. Sanday revised his views about the apocalyptic element in Jesus' teaching in a later article (1911), where he rather backtracked on his earlier enthusiasm for Schweitzer's views. He did not discuss the secrecy elements explicitly here, but the logic of his view would suggest a return to the position of his 1904 article.

27 Cf. Sanday's earlier view (n. 25 above); J. Weiss, Bousset and Wernle as in n. 21 above; Peake, 1924, 66f; Rawlinson, 1925, 262; Taylor, 1952, 377 (though he appears to criticize this view on p. 123); O. Cullmann, *The Christology of the New Testament* (ET London: SCM/Philadelphia: Westminster, 1959) 124f; Moule, 1975, 241; Dunn, pp. 127f here; cf. too Manson's claim: "The messianic secret ... is not concerned with the identity of the Messiah but with the nature of his task" (1955, 220).

28 Wrede, 1971, 41f; see too Percy, 1953, 272; Minette de Tillesse, 1968, 19; Räisänen, 1976, 30. Dunn infers this from a number of different passages.

29 But if so, why does the secrecy charge come *before* Peter has rejected Jesus' teaching about the necessity of suffering? By v. 30 Peter has given no hint that he has a false idea of messiahship. Thus, contra Manson (n. 27 above), 8:30 does appear to be about the identity of the Messiah, rather than simply about the nature of his task. (8:30 is not discussed by Manson.)

30 As indeed is done by Rawlinson, Moule and Dunn (e.g. Jesus might have wished for privacy). Cullmann does not deal with the rest of Wrede's evidence. Taylor's explanation of other texts appears to be somewhat confused: see Powley, 1980. Cf. too Barbour's comment about the theory that Jesus was avoiding political ideas of messiahship: "This does not cover all the passages concerned

very effectively, and there is a remarkable lack of passages in which Jesus is reported as trying to counter possible misunderstandings" (1968, 327).

31 Cf. Bultmann's famous sentence: "Jesus' call to decision implies a Christology" (1951, 43).

32 Cf. Räisänen, 1976, 32. See too Bultmann's critique (1951, 32) and also Strecker, pp. 51–3 here, where this claim is given further backing. If this claim can be established, then it renders questionable all attempts to see the secrecy texts as basically historical: cf. Fuller, 1963, 94f. There is, however, a danger of circularity in the argument: a secrecy text is said to be redactional because the secrecy motif is Marcan, but the secret is only said to be Marcan because all the secrecy texts are redactional. Vocabulary statistics are perhaps a better guide (cf. Luz's article here).

33 Cf. Lohmeyer, 1963, 41. E.g. 1:44; 5:43; 8:26 are taken as pre-Marcan, whilst 1:34; 7:36; 9:9 are taken as redactional.

34 1963, 25 (on 1:11), 28 (on 1:12f), etc.

35 Ibid., 5–7.

36 See Percy, 1953, 282–6; Burkill, 1961, 206–13; Minette de Tillesse, 1968, 30f; Horstmann, 1969, 111f.

37 First in Justin's *Dialogue with Trypho*, 8.

38 4 Ezra is to be dated *c.*100 A.D. The date of the Similitudes of Enoch (i.e. chaps. 37–71, which is the part containing the references to the "Son of Man") is uncertain. So far, however, no parts of this section of 1 Enoch have been found at Qumran, although fragments from elsewhere in the book have been discovered. This must, therefore, cast some doubt on whether the Similitudes are pre-Christian.

39 The parallelism would be better if in 1 Enoch, Enoch could be identified as the Son of Man whilst on earth. However, Sjöberg rejected this interpretation, claiming that in chap. 71, Enoch *becomes* the Son of Man only after leaving the earth (Sjöberg, 1955, 125 n. 1).

40 Cf. n. 32 above.

41 See p. 130 here; cf. Moule, 1975, 242f.

42 Cf. Räisänen, 1976, 32f. The issues of historicity and Mark's theology are logically separable: what is theologically important for Mark is not *ipso facto* unhistorical. Cf. Barbour's comment quoted in n. 17 above.

43 Bultmann, 1951, 32; 1963, 347; 1964, 41.

44 See Strecker, pp. 50f here.

45 Manson, 1955, 212, is somewhat misleading when he appeals to Dibelius and claims that a distinction must be drawn between the manner and the fact of the cure, and that 5:43 etc. apply to only the former. In fact, Dibelius does make this distinction, but claims that texts like 5:43 are about the fact, and *not* just about the manner, of the cure; Dibelius thought that they were patently unhistorical and therefore part of Mark's messianic secret.

46 See pp. 44–8 here. Also Weiss, 1903, 58 (for those parts of the text which are not historical); Wernle, 1907, 115; Bousset's later view, 1970, 107f; Lightfoot, 1935, 66–76; Grant, 1943, 161f; Nineham, 1963, 31f; Haenchen, 1968, 133f; also, in

part, Minette de Tillesse, 1968, 323f. Cf. too Boobyer, 1960, who says that the secret sets out to explain not the Jews' rejection of Jesus, but God's rejection of the Jews. In Burkill's view Mark also has a tendency to portray the earthly Jesus in the full glare of a divine epiphany, as in the Fourth Gospel, and this leads to some "strain" on the secret. (Cf. Burkill, 1961, 196f; 1963, 188–209). This tension in Mark is similar to that postulated by Wrede; but whereas for the latter the two views were ascribed to distinct streams of tradition, Burkill appears to postulate two radically different views in Mark's own redaction.

47 Hence one must not confuse Wrede's view with the apologetic theory, as is done by, for example, Cullmann, 1959 (n. 27), 124f; Vielhauer, 1965, 201; Kee, 1977, 168.

48 For this standard critique of the apologetic theory, see Percy, 1953, 281; Sjöberg, 1955, 117f; Räisänen, 1976, 35f; see further, Dahl's essay here, p. 29f.

49 But see Theissen, 1974, 220.

50 See Luz's essay here; also Tagawa, 1966, and Roloff, 1969 (see n. 79 below); Minette de Tillesse, 1968, 51, 111, 180, 251, etc.; also Percy, 1953, 289, referring to 4:40f; 8:32f; 9:32.

51 See Powley, 1969, 309.

52 Ebeling, 1939, 133; cf. the comment of Koch, 1975, 66.

53 See Strecker, p. 58 here; also Räisänen, 1976, 115.

54 Percy, 1953, 299.

55 Cf. Kertelge, 1970, 191ff; also those listed in n. 61 below.

56 As recognized by Percy himself (1953, 298); also Räisänen, 1976, 44.

57 See Ambrozic, 1972, 28f.

58 See Vielhauer, 1965, 200; Strecker, p. 55 here; for a fuller discussion of Schreiber's views, see E. Best, *The Temptation and the Passion – The Marcan Soteriology* (Cambridge: CUP, 1965) 125–32.

59 Cf. Marxsen, 1968, 137; also Glasswell, 1965b, 157: "The theme of the messianic secret stands over against false approaches to history or miracle which would preclude the choice of faith and forget that this is based on the Gospel and not on anything to do with the history itself."

60 Cf. also Glasswell, 1980. For Glasswell, the secret's significance is that it brings out the true relationship between history and the gospel as one of constant tension: neither can be dissolved into the other, but the two cannot be separated. The historical Jesus is the basis and presupposition of the gospel, but the preaching of the gospel and the corresponding commitment of faith are not dispensable.

61 See also Vielhauer, 1965, 213f; Luz p. 87 here; Schreiber, 1961, 158f; J. M. Robinson, 1962, 203f; Koester, 1971, 189; Keck, 1966, 368; Fuller, 1965, 228; Betz, 1968, 124; Minette de Tillesse, 1968, 321ff; Ambrozic, 1972, 99; Lambrecht, 1973, 273; Koch, 1975, 186; Anderson, 1976, 94f, 216.

62 See, for example, Keck, 1966; Minette de Tillesse, 1968, 278, 319ff; Lambrecht, 1973; also the essays here by W. C. Robinson and Dahl.

63 For the importance of the "ending" of any literary work as giving meaning and coherence to the whole, see Kermode, 1967. However, it should be noted that this claim about the literary function of the secret within Mark is quite indepen-

dent of the question of the historicity of the secret: cf. nn. 17, 42 above. Also the possibility that the cross constitutes the literary "ending" of the story does not necessarily mean that the secret itself is thought of as ended: cf. the difference between Conzelmann and Strecker noted above.

64 So, for example, Schreiber, Vielhauer, Fuller, Koester, Keck, Luz, Schweizer; also Weeden, 1971.

65 See p. 88 here. Luz has recently attempted to reconstruct more precisely the views of the pre-Marcan tradition in "Das Jesusbild der vormarkinischen Tradition", in G. Strecker (ed.), *Jesus Christus in Historie und Theologie* (Festschrift for H. Conzelmann. Tübingen: Mohr, 1975) 347–74.

66 For attempts to isolate pre-Marcan traditions, especially in the miracle stories, which present the view which Mark may be trying to correct, see L. E. Keck, "Mk 3,7–12 and Mark's Christology", *JBL* 84 (1965) 341–58; P. J. Achtemeier, "Toward the Isolation of Pre-Markan Miracle Catenae", *JBL* 89 (1970) 265–91, and "The Origin and Function of the Pre-Marcan Miracle Catenae", *JBL* 91 (1972) 198–221; Kuhn, 1971, 191ff.

67 See especially Conzelmann and Glasswell.

68 See Räisänen, 1976, 42; also W. C. Robinson's article here.

69 See the articles of Moule and Dunn; also Manson, 1955, 212: "No voice from Heaven has declared that all the injunctions to secrecy in Mark spring from the same motive, and there is no reason on earth why we should suppose that they do."

70 See Tyson, p. 36 here; cf. too Kuby, 1958.

71 See Bultmann, 1963, 258; Schreiber, 1961, 177–9; Tagawa, 1966, 174ff; Trocmé, 1975, 120ff; J. D. Crossan, "Mark and the Relatives of Jesus", *NovT* 15 (1973) 81–113; Kelber, 1974.

72 A similar theory, i.e. that Mark's presentation of the disciples is wholly negative, is given by Kelber, 1974. However, according to Kelber, the opponents of Mark (represented by the disciples in the story) err not so much in their Christology as in their eschatological beliefs.

73 Wrede, 1971, 106; see too Catchpole's review of Wrede (n. 3), 56f.

74 Cf. D. R. Catchpole, "The Fearful Silence of the Women at the Tomb", *Journal of Theology for Southern Africa* 18 (1977) 3–10.

75 See Meye, 1967, and Räisänen, 1976, 136, who refer to texts such as Mark 1:17; 3:14f; 6:7–13. Weeden, 1971, 168, thinks that these give the opponents' views of the disciples.

76 Best, 1977, 393f, points out that where the disciples do oppose Jesus, it is by no means exclusively with reference to the question of Christology. For further discussion of Weeden, see Schweizer, 1973; C. J. A. Hickling, "A Problem of Method in Gospel Research", *Religious Studies* 10 (1974) 339–46.

77 E.g. as guarantors of the Church's tradition of Jesus' words (Meye, 1967); as representatives of the later Church and examples for later Christians, partly to be followed (Peter's confession), partly to take warning from (Peter's rejection of Jesus' way of the cross) (Hawkin, 1972); as examples for the community to show God's love as refusing to give up even after human failure (Best, 1977).

78 See Focant, 1975; also Räisänen, 1976, 136.

79 See pp. 75ff here. Similarly Roloff, 1969, distinguishes three motifs: the silencing of the demons is taken over from the tradition and should be seen as no more than a standard feature of exorcism stories (cf. n. 20 above); the commands to silence after the miracles are to be interpreted in the light of their being disobeyed (hence as Luz); only the commands to silence addressed to the disciples are really part of the messianic secret, and this shows an historical awareness that the disciples receive instruction from the earthly Jesus, but they can only understand it after Easter. (Hence Roloff is close here to the interpretation of Percy and Strecker.) Roloff's threefold division of the texts is also that of Tagawa, 1966. Tagawa interprets the first two groups (commands to the demons and to those who have been healed) as Roloff does. However, he sees the motif of the disciples' incomprehension as part of a polemic against the Jerusalem church.

80 Pesch, 1977, 36–45.

81 Cf. the recent study by Kermode, 1979. However, despite its title, Kermode's book does not set out to deal with the texts in Mark usually associated with the messianic secret, apart from Mark 4:11f. Kermode deals more with the general opaqueness of all narrative, rather than with the secrecy elements in Mark's Gospel. His book is suggestive rather than definitive, and there are clearly further insights to be gained from considering Mark from a literary-critical point of view. See review article by H. D. Betz, *Journal of Religion* (1982).

82 Cf. the recent study of Mark's Gospel by Kee, 1977. According to Kee, the secret is related to the confidence of Mark's community that its hopes will be realized (1977, 174f).

# 1
# *The Purpose of Mark's Gospel**

NILS ALSTRUP DAHL

The so-called messianic secret (better: the Christ-mystery) is not a literary device intended to maintain suspense by keeping something hidden from the reader until he learns the solution of the enigma. The Christ-mystery is a secret only for those persons who appear in the book. The readers know the point of the story from the very beginning: it is the gospel of Jesus Christ. They know that Jesus was the stronger one who would come after John and baptize with the Holy Spirit, the one in whose name they themselves have been baptized. It has never been concealed from them that during his entire earthly life Jesus was the beloved Son in whom God was well pleased. They know the answer to the disciples' astonished question: "Who can this be?" They know that when Jesus died, forsaken by men and by God, it happened in order that the Scriptures should be fulfilled: the Son of man gave his life as a ransom for many. Mark is not presenting the solution to something which has been an unanswered riddle; he is emphasizing the mysterious character of something with which his readers are familiar.

Wrede claimed that the messianic secret was an attempt to harmonize the earlier view that Jesus became Messiah only at the resurrection with the later view that Jesus' earthly life had a messianic character. This understanding of the messianic secret as a transitional device hardly explains the origin of the motif and certainly does not explain its function in Mark.[1] More widespread than Wrede's explanation of the messianic secret is the view that it is apologetic in character.[2] According to this interpretation, the injunctions to silence and the theme of divine hardening of hearts explain Jesus' rejection by his own people though he was the Messiah and a great worker of miracles. But if the concern had been apologetic, one would have expected Matthew and Luke to have made greater use

* First published in English in *Jesus in the Memory of the Early Church* by N. A. Dahl (1976) 55–60. Original publication in Swedish (1958).

of the idea. In fact, the other two synoptics do have an apologetic tendency, each in its own way, which it is difficult to find in Mark. Further, Israel's unbelief does not play the role in the second Gospel that the theory presupposes. Matthew shows how Jesus' life and passion are the foundation of the Church's existence in its opposition to the synagogue, and at the same time he emphasizes that the new people stand under the command of Jesus and will appear before his judgement seat. Luke–Acts tells how God's promises to Israel were fulfilled in Jesus, and how the salvation promised to Israel was extended to the Gentiles. In Mark, the portrayal of the Jews is more differentiated than in the other Gospels. The relation to the Jewish people is neither a present conflict as in Matthew nor a problem of salvation history as in Luke.

Mark presupposes the Church and the Gentile mission, but his interest is concentrated on Jesus himself. The contrast between "you" and "those outside" in Mark 4:11 cannot be identified with the contrast between the Church and the synagogue. It has to do more generally with the division between believers and non-believers. Together with the injunctions to silence and the messianic secret in general, the distinction between public teaching in parables and esoteric interpretations serves to elucidate the gospel's character as a revealed mystery. Jesus and his word become genuine revelation and salvation only for the chosen circle to whom the secret is given.

The connection between the messianic secret and the crucifixion must be different from that which proponents of the apologetic theory have supposed. Mark's stress on the mystery of Jesus' life must be closely associated with the peculiar character of the Marcan passion story. Mark does not give prominence to Jesus' sovereign power in the midst of suffering as do Matthew and John, nor does he portray Jesus as the exemplary martyr as Luke does. In Mark, the picture of Jesus as the hidden, contradicted and misunderstood Messiah reaches its high point in the passion story. There Jesus is depicted as the rejected one who was betrayed, deserted and denied by his own, slandered, condemned, spat upon and ridiculed, mocked as he hung on the cross, even by those who were crucified with him. Not the physical suffering but the expulsion from human fellowship is stressed again and again. Even his cry in deepest need and loneliness, "My God, my God ... !" elicits only a crude joke. The concealing of Jesus' messiahship is not an apologetic theory intended to explain how Jesus was rejected. The case is just the reverse. In Mark, the historical fact that Jesus was spurned by the majority of Jews serves to illustrate the mysterious character of the revelation and salvation given in him. It has to do with "what no eye has seen, nor ear heard, nor the heart of man conceived, what God has prepared for those who love him".

Partly in line with the interpretation advanced here, H. J. Ebeling has made the evangelist's kerygmatic intention the basis for his explanation of the messianic secret in Mark.[3] He believes the secret to be a literary device which serves to stress the greatness of the revelation in which the readers participate as they hear the Christian message. Against this interpretation it has been rightly maintained that Ebeling has overemphasized the purely literary at the expense of content and religious meaning. It has been further objected that it is not legitimate to place the evangelist's kerygmatic intention in any exclusive contrast to historicity.[4] Ebeling writes in a somewhat inflated style, without sufficient precision, which is shown not least by his use of the fashionable word "kerygmatic". The worthwhile element lies in the emphasis that there must be a close connection between the messianic secret and the evangelist's "message" or purpose. But he misses the mark because his understanding of revelation and proclamation as an always contemporary call to decision is one-sided. Mark writes for those who are already in the Church and have received the secret of God's Kingdom as a gift. His goal is not to persuade readers to believe in the message but to remind them of what is contained in it in order that they might understand what has been given to them. The purpose is not kerygmatic in the word's narrower sense, but rather theological or – to coin a word – anamnetic.[5]

That the evangelist has Christian readers in mind is evident especially from his description of the relation of the disciples to the Christ-mystery. As often pointed out, it is a two-sided relationship. The secret of the Kingdom of God is given to the disciples; they recognize that Jesus is the Messiah and are instructed concerning the necessity of suffering. An inner circle receives special revelations. Nevertheless, we constantly hear that the disciples lack faith and do not understand. There are certain hints that their insight gradually increases; but even so, they fail in the hour of crisis. Contrasted to those outside, the disciples are the recipients of revelation. Despite this fact, they form the dark background against which the figure of Christ appears. Mark does not go as far as the author of the letter of Barnabas, who says that the disciples were sinful beyond measure (5:9). But Mark's picture of the disciples can also serve to illustrate Jesus' words: "I came not to call the righteous, but sinners." Not their own fitness, but Jesus' call and God's gift make them

Jesus' disciples and recipients of the mystery of God's Kingdom. Not because of their fidelity, but despite their failures, they became after the resurrection the bearers of Jesus' message and the kernel of the Church.

Mark's picture of the disciples cannot without qualification be regarded as typical of his view of Christians. He markedly contrasts time prior to the resurrection with time after the resurrection. It was during the time of Jesus' earthly life that the miracles, the messiahship, and the necessity of suffering were to be kept hidden; during this time the disciples lacked understanding and faith. Throughout Mark's Gospel, the messianic secret expresses an understanding of the "history of revelation" (Percy), according to which the decisive and complete revelation of the mystery, the realization of God's saving plan, first occurred with Jesus' death and resurrection. The Easter events place a dividing line between the period when Jesus lived as the hidden and misunderstood Messiah, and the time when he is openly proclaimed as the Crucified and Risen One. But this does not mean that the possibility for failure among Jesus' followers has ceased, that the dark picture of the disciples' behaviour during Jesus' life on earth was only to be a foil for an all the more radiant picture of the Church which lives in faith in the risen Lord. The conclusion of the Gospel shows on the contrary that even when the message that Jesus is risen is proclaimed by angels, those who hear can react in a manner which is no more adequate than that of the disciples when Jesus was among them.

If it were the case that the disciples' misunderstanding only provided contrast to the understanding which is now granted to the Church, the same should apply to the disciples' inability to work miracles.[6] But even if we retain the full force of the sayings concerning the boundless possibilities open to believers, it is unlikely that Mark thought these possibilities were realized in the Church. His emphasis on the disciples' shortcomings cannot be fully explained as stemming from Mark's view of the "history of revelation". The additional feature is paraenetic. This paraenetic concern was already present in tradition, most clearly in the Gethsemane narrative: "Watch and pray that you may not enter into temptation." Mark makes it something of a continuing theme. The members of the Church who have partaken of the full revelation and salvation must see to it that they do not fall short, misunderstand and fail as the disciples did in the time before the resurrection. Ferdinand Kattenbusch once wrote: "The Twelve are 'authorities' for the learning church, *types* for the celebrating 'church'."[7] With reference to Mark one might add: they are examples intended to serve as a warning to a complacent Church lacking in faith.

What is said here about the Christ-mystery in Mark can be illuminated by analagous conceptions in the epistles. Ephesians and Colossians, and texts like 1 Cor. 2:6–16 and 1 Pet. 1:1–12 imply that the presentation of the gospel's content as a mystery had its setting in preaching to the community rather than in missionary proclamation. But there is a significant difference. The epistles speak of the mystery which was hidden from angels, powers and principalities. But according to Mark, the demons knew who Jesus was. Especially in the Pauline letters, the Christ-mystery is placed within a cosmic framework which is missing in Mark. But the difference has to do mostly with the forms of perception. If one enquires as to what function the conceptions have, the similarity becomes more pronounced. The ignorance of the angelic powers underlines the hiddenness of God's plan, now revealed in Christ for man's salvation. Mark achieves the same end by stressing that the demons were forbidden to make Christ known though they recognized Jesus to be God's Son, while men did not understand the secret of his person and suffering.

In the epistles too the purpose is practical and paraenetic: Christians are urged to realize the greatness of the revealed mystery and to conform their lives to the pattern provided by the salvation granted them. In 1 Corinthians 2 Paul speaks of God's mysterious wisdom which was hidden from the rulers of this age but is revealed to Christians through the Spirit. Paul's stress on this wisdom contained in the word of the cross, which he was unable to unfold fully in Corinth, is meant to put to shame those Christians who are quarrelling and fighting, who brag about their leaders and want to be great themselves. It is not inconceivable that a similar concern lies behind Mark's emphasis on the messianic secret and related concepts.

## NOTES

1 Cf. the critical objections of Ebeling, Percy and Sjöberg.

2 The explanation offered by T. A. Burkill in a series of articles and in his book, *Mysterious Revelation*, is a variant of this theory. It has been criticized by Ebeling, Percy and Sjöberg.

3 Ebeling, 1939.

4 Percy, 288ff; Sjöberg, 118ff.

5 Cf. my essay, "Anamnesis", *Jesus in the Memory of the Early Church* (Minneapolis: Augsburg, 1976) 11–29.

6 J. Coutts, "The Authority of Jesus and of the Twelve in St Mark's Gospel", *JTS* 8 (1957) 111–18, has observed that the disciples' inability to perform miracles should be added to the features noted by Wrede.

7 *Festgabe für Karl Müller* (1922) 347, n. 1. Cf. O. Linton, "Das Problem der Urkirche", Uppsala univeritets årsskrift (1932) 96–100.

# 2
# *The Blindness of the Disciples in Mark**

JOSEPH B. TYSON

## I

The blindness of the disciples is usually regarded as a device of Mark and as part of his messianic secret motif. William Wrede, in 1901, said that the motif of the messianic secret in Mark was the evangelist's explanation of the fact that Jesus was not accepted as Messiah during his lifetime but was proclaimed as Messiah after the death and resurrection. Wrede felt that the facts of history demanded the conclusion that Jesus did not proclaim himself as Messiah, but that the disciples did; Mark could not, of course, say this directly; so he explained the phenomenon of silence as an intentional secret. The explanation of the purpose of parables in chap. 4 is one clue to this, as Mark 9:9 is perhaps the keystone. The very purpose of Jesus' parables is to hide the secret of his nature. The demons recognize the nature of Jesus, but Jesus commands them to be silent. The disciples partially understand who Jesus is, but they, too, are commanded to keep silence. The hostility and opposition of the Jewish authorities to Jesus is easily explained by the supposition that God had intentionally blinded them to the reality of Jesus.

Mark seems to work out this theory on three levels:

1 The demons recognize Jesus, but they are commanded to be silent.[1]
2 The disciples partially recognize Jesus, but they are commanded to be silent.[2]
3 The Jewish authorities fail to recognize Jesus because they have been blinded.[3]

It is the second level that engages our attention at this point. The disciples are commanded to be silent, but their recognition of Jesus

*First published in *JBL* 80 (1961) 261–8.

is only partial, due to their blindness and their hardness of heart.[4] Moreover, their incomplete understanding is actually a misunderstanding of the nature of Jesus. When we look at the incidents related by Mark in which the disciples fail to understand, then it will appear that this element is not properly a part of the messianic secret motif. It is not as if the disciples had discerned the nature of Jesus but are prohibited from broadcasting it, but it is that the disciples have a wrong conception about his nature.

There are many instances of the disciples' blindness – they do not understand the stilling of the sea (4:41), the feeding of the five thousand (6:52), Jesus' attitude towards children (10:13ff), the saying about the rich entering the Kingdom (10:23); they are characteristically unable to understand parables (4:1–20, 33f).

Above all, however, the misunderstanding of the disciples is connected with Jesus' threefold prediction of suffering. It is profitable at this point to look briefly at the actual contents of these three predictions.

The first prediction (Mark 8:31–3) is intimately connected with the confession of Peter in 8:27–30. This is the first indication we have that the disciples suspect Jesus to be the Messiah. Throughout the narrative, Peter is the spokesman, but he clearly seems to be speaking for the group. Although it is not crystal-clear that Jesus accepts the confession of Peter at this point, he moves quickly into an introduction of the necessity of his own suffering. To this Peter expresses not only surprise but some indignation. Jesus rebukes Peter in very harsh words, equating his point of view with that of Satan.

The second prediction of suffering in 9:30–2 is substantially the same as that of 8:31–3. The prediction is followed by the words, "But they (the disciples) did not understand the saying, and they were afraid to ask him." The following pericope in Mark tells us that the disciples had been discussing their relative greatness, giving Jesus a chance to discourse on true greatness.

In the third prediction in 10:32–4 we have much the same pattern, except that the prediction of suffering is much more detailed. Nothing is said in this paragraph about the misunderstanding of the disciples, but the following paragraph tells the story of the request of James and John for places of authority when Jesus comes into his Kingdom.[5]

In these three predictions of suffering, not only does Mark indicate that the disciples misunderstood the nature of Jesus, but he also sees this misunderstanding as of two specific kinds: (1) No understanding of the necessity of Jesus' sufferings; and (2) no understanding of their own position in the community. The point is this: Mark is not here saying that the disciples understood that Jesus was Messiah and were commanded not to broadcast it; rather he is saying that they completely misunderstood the nature of Jesus' messiahship, not understanding it as a suffering messiahship but as a royal messiahship which would issue in benefits for themselves.

## II

Now it will be our intention to examine both of these "misunderstood elements" to see exactly what Mark would seem to be driving at. If the case is simply that Mark is trying to explain the fact that Jesus was not understood to be the Messiah during his lifetime, that is one thing. But this does not seem to be the case. Rather Mark seems to be trying to indicate that the disciples really misunderstood the position of Jesus. Why would Mark say this? The most obvious answer is that Mark is aware of a significant difference between his own point of view and that of the disciples.[6] To Mark the disciples' understanding of Jesus' messiahship is a misunderstanding. If Mark 9:9 indicates that it was only after the resurrection that the disciples began preaching the messiahship of Jesus, then the predictions of suffering indicate just what kind of messiahship they understood and preached.

There would be two important elements in their preaching:

1 It would be a preaching which (to Mark) did not take full account of the *necessity* of suffering. Mark's portrayal of the events makes it clear that the disciples did not really anticipate the suffering and death of Jesus. They fled the scene. Peter denied his relationship to Jesus. All indications in Mark point to the probability that they had not been warned about the death of Jesus.[7] They, in fact, did not expect the death of Jesus because they had not been warned of it. This probably means that the predictions of suffering in Mark are quite artificial and bear no resemblance to authentic history. But does it mean any more than that? Does it mean that even after the death/resurrection the disciples did not understand the profound meaning of the suffering?

It has been a most difficult position to maintain that the disciples did not understand the necessity of Jesus' sufferings, because it is difficult to see how the disciples could have preached the messiahship of Jesus without making some sense out of his death. How could a crucified criminal be the saviour of the world? This, it is said, would be a considerable stumbling block to Christian proclamation. The Christian preacher would meet this stumbling block from the very first and would find it necessary to explain the relation of death to messiahship as a first step in gaining acceptance for this new message. But this is not quite the problem it might at first seem; for the disciples were, from the beginning, preaching, not simply a death, but a death/resurrection. The resurrection is the only answer that is necessary. If the speech of Peter in Acts 2 can be regarded as, in any way, authentic, it represents precisely this point of view. "This Jesus whom you crucified, God has raised up and has made both Lord and Christ." Here is no attempt to explain the necessity of the death of Jesus. It is simply treated as an historical fact which illustrates the cruelty and stupidity of the Jewish authorities. But there is no hint that the death is necessary for the messiahship. The very opposite is the more nearly true. Jesus is the Christ in spite of, not because of, the death. The resurrection answers all questions.[8]

By calling attention to this deficiency on the part of the disciples, Mark is, to some extent, condemning them. He sees quite clearly the necessity of Jesus' suffering and death, but the disciples did not. Mark seems to have been quite aware that he is introducing something into the Christian tradition that was not a part of the preaching of the disciples. Nor do we have to look far for the basis of Mark's point of view. Whether or not Mark and Paul represent identical points of view, they both place great importance on the necessity of Jesus' death.

2 When we come to the second element in the disciples' misunderstanding, it becomes quite clear that Mark thinks of himself as holding a different view of messiahship from that of the disciples. Hence Mark calls attention to the fact that the disciples did not understand what was to be their own relationship to the community. This, in Mark, forms a part of the second and third predictions of suffering. The second prediction is followed by a report that the disciples had been conversing with one another about their relative importance in the Kingdom of God (9:33–7). This seems to amplify the statement in 9:32 that the disciples did not understand. No, says Mark, the disciples did not understand about Jesus' coming death, and this illustrates it. Likewise, although there is no direct statement in the third prediction of suffering, the saying is followed by the request of James and John for the chief seats when Jesus comes into his Kingdom (10:35–45). The third prediction of suffering is exactly

parallel to the second in idea, though not in specific content. Both are followed by a story in which the disciples discuss their own importance.

Whatever historical episode may lie behind the narrative, the important thing is to discover the reason for its presence in Mark. That reason seems to be Mark's feeling that the disciples understood Jesus in terms of a royal messiahship, and that this is simply a misunderstanding. The question of rank can only come up among the disciples if the disciples accept Jesus as a royal Messiah. Mark is saying that this is the way the disciples conceived of Jesus.[9]

Now, one can admit that this was the thinking of the disciples before the death of Jesus, but would this have been the case afterward? The first thing that can be said is that there is nothing to show that the early disciples did not have such an idea. It is true that Jesus did not exercise messianic functions during his lifetime, but he was now the Christ, and he would return soon to establish his Kingdom.[10] On the positive side must be noted the fact that there was in the Jerusalem church a kind of family dynasty set up which began with James, the brother of Jesus, and, according to Hegesippus as reported in Eusebius, passed to James' cousin, Simeon bar Clopas,[11] who was executed for being of the house of David.[12] Eusebius records a total of fifteen members of this family who held the position of "bishop" of Jerusalem.[13]

There is every indication that the Christianity of this church, which probably included most of the original disciples, took the form of a mildly modified Judaism, Paul's controversies with the church reveal a great deal about Jerusalem Christianity, but two things in particular: (1) that there was something of a struggle for power which attempted to keep Paul within bounds on the basis that he was not an apostle of Jesus during Jesus' lifetime; and (2) that the leaders of the church really wished to require circumcision and obedience to the kosher food laws for incoming Christians.[14] The distinctive element in the thinking of this group is belief in the future messiahship of Jesus. We must recognize that, if it were not for Mark and Paul, we would have to assume that the messiahship in which the disciples believed was a royal messiahship. That is to say, if there were no specific indications one way or the other, we would have no alternative but to assume that by Messiah the disciples meant a new Davidic king. But the fact is that we do have evidence: (1) the family of Jesus is in control of the church at Jerusalem from the very earliest period. The attempt is made to establish a dynasty of the family of Jesus, a royal family waiting for the return of the king.[15] (2) Other disciples seem to have high-ranking offices in the Jerusalem church. Those "reputed to be pillars" make it very difficult for a free lance like Paul to gain any kind of authority in the church. (3) The Jerusalem church seems to have no desire to initiate a mission to Gentiles. What does messiahship mean to Gentiles? Jesus is to be the new king of Judah, and this will have only an indirect bearing on the gentile world. Basically, the messiahship of Jesus is meaningful only for the Jewish people. (4) Therefore, there seems also to be no question in the Jerusalem church about the abandonment of long-established Jewish practices. The future messiahship of Jesus only makes it all the more necessary to carry on the best religious principles one knows in as pure a fashion as possible until his return. It cannot be imagined, of course, that the teaching of Jesus would not have been remembered and would have had no real influence over the practices of the church. But over against this are the facts which necessitate the view that Jerusalem Christianity entailed only a mildly modified Judaism. The major modification was the vivid expectation of the return of Jesus as a royal Messiah.

## III

Now we are in a position to see where Mark stands in relation to the Jerusalem church, whose point of view seems to be represented in the Gospel by the disciples. Mark is aware of two things: (1) He is aware that the death of Jesus is much more than an historical fact. He feels that it has redemptive significance. Jesus gives his life as "a ransom for many".[16] (2) Mark is also aware that Jesus' messiahship is not simply a nationalistic royal messiahship. For this reason he makes relatively little of the "Son of David" theology.[17] Accordingly he calls attention to the fact that Jesus' family had no understanding of him and no little hostility towards him.[18] For this reason he twice tells of incidents in which the disciples foolishly vie with one another for some kind of reflected or delegated authority. Mark is aware, then, of a view of messiahship quite different from that of the original disciples and family of Jesus, and is aware that his own viewpoint is in some conflict with that of these original witnesses. He seems also to know that his readers recognize this conflict; therefore, he must give some explanation for it. His explanation is that the disciples did not understand, even though Jesus many times tried to explain it to them.

If it is correct that Mark's view of messiahship is different from that of the early disciples, it is necessary to ask where this later view came from. There are several possibilities:

1 It is quite possible that Mark has been influenced by Paul. We do not wish to dredge up all the old arguments for and against Pauline influence on Mark. But what we seem to have arrived at is this. In the first place, Mark seems to appreciate the significance of the death of Jesus in a much more profound way than did the disciples. Although we do not have, by any means, a complete picture of the history of early Christianity, what we do know is that Paul had a very deep appreciation of the necessity of Jesus' death. There may have been others, but there is certainly Paul. In the second place, we know that Mark does not think much of apostolic authority; that is, he does not think very highly of those who held the point of view of the Jerusalem church. Again, we do not have a complete picture of primitive church history, but we do know that if ever anyone came into conflict with the Jerusalem church it was Paul. Whether there is any historical connection between Paul and Mark or not, Mark lands on Paul's side in questioning the authority of the pillars in Jerusalem. There is enough here that we can entertain the possibility, if not the probability, that it was under the influence of Paul that Mark (and the group which Mark represents) was led to see the death of Jesus as of redemptive significance and to question the authority of the apostles.

2 It is possible that Mark represents Galilean Christianity rather than Jerusalem Christianity. Here we are obviously drawing on Ernst Lohmeyer, who maintained that the basic Christology of the Galilean church was a "Son of Man" Christology and that of the Jerusalem church was a "Son of David" Christology. Lohmeyer quite convincingly argues that Mark stands within the Galilean tradition.[19]

3 It is more than likely that it is Mark's appreciation for the gentile mission which has brought about this difference in point of view. Obviously, appreciation for the gentile mission would involve appreciation for Paul, the apostle to the Gentiles par excellence. But Mark is not limited to this. To him, Jesus is much more than a nationalistic Messiah to the Jews. He has significance for all the world, and this significance cannot involve the strait-jacket limitations imposed by a hierarchy of relatives and friends of Jesus. Mark is apparently writing from and representing the point of view of the church which is soon to become the leading church of Christendom. As a matter of fact, it is not long after the time of Mark that Rome begins to rise to a leading position among the Christian churches. In a sense, Mark's Gospel represents a challenge to the power of the Jerusalem church, which, at least in the time of Paul and probably

for a few years afterward, exercised almost unquestioned authority over the other churches. Mark is a challenge to this church and its leaders, a challenge not only of authority, but of theology. The fact that Mark feels it necessary to make this challenge indicates that even in his time the disciples enjoyed considerable prestige if not authority.[20]

In summary, Mark consciously differs from the original disciples along two lines: (1) He feels that they have a narrow view of the messiahship of Jesus which involves an inflated understanding of their own position; (2) He feels that they do not have a profound enough understanding of the significance of the death of Jesus. In this light, it is possible to maintain that the Gospel of Mark ended exactly as we now have it. Even the resurrection is not understood by Jesus' associates. They were in a position to see and to proclaim, but they told no one, for they were afraid. Although only three women are mentioned as seeing the empty tomb, surely the disciples are in Mark's mind, as 16:7 indicates. Moreover, it may be significant that Mark does not describe an appearance of the risen Jesus to the disciples. Here is the climax of the Gospel, and, although Mark looks forward to some kind of experience on the part of the "disciples and Peter", these are not the first to hear the news of Jesus' resurrection. What a strange ending for our earliest Gospel, and yet what an appropriate and significant one if one of Mark's chief purposes was to call attention to the ways in which the disciples fell short in their understanding and proclamation of the Chritian gospel.

## NOTES

1 Cf. Mark 1:23–5, 34; 3:11–12; 5:6, 7; 9:20.

2 Mark 7:36; 8:30; 9:9.

3 Cf. especially Mark 4:12.

4 Mark 6:52; 8:17.

5 Cf. Taylor, 1952, 436f. Although Taylor can find no reason to doubt the substantial historicity of the first two predictions, he does believe that, in its precision and close relationship to the passion narrative in Mark, the third is a *"vaticinium ex eventu"*.

6 Cf. Kuby, 1958, who maintains that the Gospel of Mark falls into two main divisions. The first, 1:16—8:21, deals with the failure of the disciples to understand who Jesus is. The second half, 8:22—14:72, deals with the misunderstanding of the disciples, i.e., their unwillingness to grasp the fact that the Messiah must suffer.

7 Especially the notice in Mark that prior to the arrest the leading disciples were

sleeping (14:32–42) and that upon the arrest of Jesus they fled the scene (14:50).

8 The fact that Luke also gives us a story of Philip, in which the death of Jesus is explained by the help of 2 Isaiah, need not cause us to detour from this position. The question is simply – is it possible that the disciples could have preached the messiahship of Jesus without explaining the death? The answer is that in the early chapters of Acts this possibility is opened up: that is to say, the disciples could have been preaching in just the way Mark seems to think they were preaching. In addition, Paul represents this thinking, at least in part, where he says that Jesus was "designated Son of God in power according to the Spirit of holiness by his resurrection from the dead" (Rom. 1:4).

9 Taylor, 1952, 438f, defends the historicity of Mark 10:35–40, on the grounds that the community would not create a story which discredits these disciples. Be that as it may, the point being made here is that Mark is aware that, not only in the life of Jesus, but in the life of the early Church, certain disciples felt themselves called to positions of great authority. This feeling, to Mark, must rest on their misunderstanding of the messiahship of Jesus.

10 Luke certainly is aware of this when, in Acts 1:6–7, he has the risen Christ correct the disciples who expect him at that time to "restore the kingdom to Israel".

11 Eusebius, *Eccl. hist.* 3, 11, 1.

12 Ibid., 3, 32, 3.

13 Ibid., 4, 5, 3–4.

14 Gal. 1—2.

15 Cf. S. G. F. Brandon, *The Fall of Jerusalem and the Christian Church* (London, 1951). In chap. 10 of this book Brandon states his belief that it was actually the fall of Jerusalem and the end of the Jerusalem leadership in the church which called forth the writing of the Gospel of Mark. In this light, Mark feels it necessary to make clear his own differences with the Jerusalem Christianity. Brandon here says that Mark's rejection of the "Son of David" motif is a definitive attempt to repudiate an interpretation of the status of Jesus which would connect him with the nationalistic aspiration of the Jews.

16 Mark 10:45.

17 As a matter of fact, he directly repudiates the "Son of David" theology in 12:35–7.

18 Mark 3:21, 31–5; 6:2–3.

19 *Galiläa und Jerusalem*, 26–35.

20 This point of view need not involve the question of the date of Mark, although these matters should be considered in establishing such a date. On the other hand, although the Jerusalem church did, in all probability, cease to exist after A.D. 70, it prestige would not die immediately. Brandon seems to feel that Mark's Gospel is an attempt to say what the Christian Church will now do without the Jerusalem leadership.

# 3
# *Mysterious Revelation**

T. A. BURKILL

Mark's Gospel is not an essay in scientific biography, but a religious document which was written for the edification of believers. As we gather from its superscription, the evangelist is concerned to depict the life of Jesus as the earthly career of the Messiah, the Son of God, and it is interesting to find that the declarations of the heavenly voice and the confessions of the demons are supplemented in the later part of the Gospel by a Jew's testimony to the messiahship at 8:29 and by a Gentile's testimony to the divine Sonship at 15:39. Despite the fundamentally divine character of its central figure, however, the gospel story is not an epic of unrelieved triumph and continuous success, for it relates how Jesus was rejected by his own people and crucified by the Gentiles, and Mark evidently seeks to overcome the difficulty thus raised by holding that the true status of Jesus was a predetermined secret. The Master was not accepted as the Messiah, and the evangelist maintains that it was an integral part of the divine purpose that he should not have been so accepted. Hence in the second Gospel Jesus is represented as deliberately concealing the truth from the public by the injunctions to silence and by the cryptology of parabolical teaching.

Accordingly, Christianity was (as it remains) essentially a paradoxical religion which had to make room in its total interpretation of messiahship for the shame of the crucifixion. The situation demanded that the Church should reconcile the indubitable fact of the humiliation of Jesus with its ardent faith in his ultimate supremacy as the plenipotentiary of God. Indeed, it was precisely the task of synthesizing such opposing conceptions in a coherent scheme of thought that constituted the main problem of apostolic Christology. The earliest solution, which finds characteristic expression in the writings of Paul, appears to have been that the Messiah's sufferings were a necessary prelude to his final manifestation in

* First published in *Mysterious Revelation* by T. A. Burkill (1963) 319–24.

glory. Mark, however, refuses to regard the messianic glory purely as an object of anticipation to be realized in the future and, in some measure, he considers that it is already evident amid all the lowliness and shame of the Master's life on earth. But in so far as the Church's historical traditions concerning the career of its founder are evaluated from such a standpoint, the difficulty raised by the rejection of Jesus becomes all the more acute; and this helps us to understand why the evangelist emphasizes the secret character of the messiahship.

Broadly speaking, Mark seems to distinguish four principal stages or periods in the historical realization of God's plan of salvation: the period of preparation, which comes to an end with the imprisonment of the appointed forerunner; the period of the incarnate life, which is characterized by suffering and obscurity; the post-resurrection period of enlightenment, in which the gospel of the crucified Messiah is publicly proclaimed by the Church; and the period of eschatological fulfilment, which will be gloriously inaugurated by the Son of Man at his awaited parousia. It is not to be supposed, however, that the evangelist presents us with a systematic body of doctrine concerning these periods and the manner of their interconnection. He is much less a master of his material than the fourth evangelist, for example, and this is not surprising seeing that he was apparently the first writer to respond to the Church's increasing need for a connected account of the ministry.

But there can be little doubt regarding Mark's fundamental attitude. Convinced that Jesus is the Messiah, he takes the view that the Lord's humiliation represents the pledge or guarantee of his triumph in glory which is subsequently to be made manifest. It is as though the soteriological process were governed by a principle of divine retribution which ultimately effects a reversal of the situation existing during the period of the earthly ministry. Heavenly exaltation is the reward of self-abnegation. The evangelist therefore contemplates the sufferings of Jesus and the tribulations of the Church in the light of a revelation in glory, and yet, since the reward always comes after the humiliation, there is a break or rift in the soteriological process. Thus, in an important sense, Mark's thought is basically bipolar. The sufferings and the glory belong to different epochs, and the relationship between them has the appearance of being no more intimate than that which obtains between means and end. They are not brought together in the unity of a single conception as they are, for example, in the Fourth Gospel, where the notion of the cost of the passion has almost disappeared.

On the other hand, there is a counter-tendency at work which militates against the bipolarity of the evangelist's fundamental position and induces him to represent the life of Jesus as the locus of secret revelation. Apparently, he is not completely satisfied with the doctrine that the humiliation of the Messiah is the appointed means to his future triumph, and thus he comes to attach a greater degree of intrinsic importance to the incarnate life than seems to be allowed in the epistles of Paul, who betrays little or no interest in the actual details of the Lord's earthly ministry. Probably the delay in the arrival of the parousia helped to bring about the new emphasis. But in whatever manner the change is to be accounted for, Mark undoubtedly goes some way towards closing the gap, as it were, between the notion of the Messiah's humiliation and that of his supremacy, or towards overcoming the bipolarity of what appears to be his primary philosophical position. In the story of the transfiguration, for instance, the veil of the flesh is temporarily withdrawn, and the three most intimate disciples are privileged to behold their Master as he really is and in the form in which he will be made manifest to the world when he comes again finally to establish the Kingdom of God with great power and glory.

But the counter-tendency in question is more pronounced in some passages than in others, and, whenever it becomes particularly strong, Mark is inclined to overstep the limits prescribed by his doctrine of the secret and to delineate the incarnate life openly in terms of the apostolic faith. Hence certain passages convey the impression that the true nature of Jesus is reaching out for some definite form of articulate expression which, however, it cannot yet receive; in the stories of the triumphal entry and of the anointing at Bethany, for example, the evangelist's belief in the reality of the messiahship is apparently pressing for overt recognition in the narrative, thereby putting great strain on the requirement of secrecy. And, notably, in the account of the nocturnal trial the pressure exerted by the evangelist's conviction subjects his doctrine of the secret to a strain which it cannot withstand, the result being that in 14:62 there is actually a disclosure of the fact of the messiahship outside the circle of the initiated. Forsaken by his followers and confronted by his enemies in all their worldly might, Jesus gives open confession to his messianic status and confidently declares that his judges shall see the Son of Man coming with the clouds of heaven. Thus something of the supernatural glory of the parousia lights up the darkest depths of the humiliation to which the passion narrative bears witness; and we are presented with what is, from one point of view, the most striking exemplification in the entire Gospel of Mark's inclination to move away from the conception of the incarnate life as the period of obscurity towards a characteristically Johannine mode of representation.

In the last-mentioned passage, however, the urge to set forth the earthly ministry directly in terms of the apostolic faith seems to be reinforced by the motive to ascribe responsibility for the crucifixion to the Jews as represented by their leaders. For, although Mark believes that the passion was provided for in God's sovereign purpose, he none the less wishes to show that the crucifixion really took place through the unwarranted hostility of the Lord's own countrymen and hence that the burden of guilt for that most terrible crime is borne by a people whose God-given privileges only serve to make their conduct the more reprehensible. The operation of such a motive naturally makes for a certain inconsistency in the evangelist's treatment of his material. As we should expect, in so far as he is concerned to emphasize the culpability of the Jews, he tends to contravene the requirement of secrecy by allowing the true nature of Jesus to come out, so to speak, into the light of day. Consequently, in Mark's representation Jesus does not always address the public in the cryptology of parables, as he is said to do in 4:34, and he does not always seek to perform his miracles in private, as he does, for example, in 5:40. On the contrary, in certain passages the fact of the messiahship is to a greater or less extent exposed to public view, and so it could be maintained that the Jews were in an inexcusable position, since they had perpetrated their crime not in ignorance but with a cognizance of that for which Jesus stood.

In Mark's interpretation, then, the life of Jesus, despite its outward show of tragic frustration, is really a continuous fulfilment of God's plan of salvation. The failure of the public to recognize the fact of the messiahship and the failure of the disciples to understand its meaning are alike provisions of the divine purpose for the redemption of humanity. But it is important to notice that the two instances of failure do not make their historical appearance in the same way. For, while the fact of the messiahship is concealed from the public by the injunctions to silence and by the teaching in parables, it is discovered by Peter at Caesarea Philippi, whereupon its implications are expounded to the twelve and something of its essential glory is made manifest to the privileged three on the occasion of the transfiguration. The veil is withdrawn in the presence of the chosen few, but they are not yet in a position to grasp the significance of the *mysterium* revealed to them. Their spiritual sight is dim, and so it must remain until the time of the Messiah's resurrection, which marks the end of the period of obscurity and the beginning of the period of enlightenment. Thus the confession at Caesarea Philippi is of importance in the evangelist's thought because it serves as a basis for further instruction which, besides preparing the mind of the reader for a right appreciation of the passion narrative, enables the disciples to receive the saving truth of the gospel from the Lord himself. For, although they cannot understand the divine word when it is communicated to them, they can retain it as authentic tradition and can thus equip themselves for their future role as apostles and pillars of the Church.

# 4

# *The Theory of the Messianic Secret in Mark's Gospel**

GEORG STRECKER

The problem of the theory of the messianic secret in Mark's Gospel is still defined in exegetical research in the terms of William Wrede's epoch-making study *The Messianic Secret*, which was first published more than sixty years ago.[1] In this book Wrede directed his attack against historicist life of Jesus research which sought to reconstruct a messianic life of Jesus on the basis of Mark's Gospel. He showed that what the evangelist was actually saying could not be interpreted psychologically, and therefore could not be verified historically: rather, it was "supernaturally" coloured. As the supernatural view of the life of Jesus went back to the faith of the community, so too, according to Wrede, the concept of the secret revelations of Jesus the Messiah was pre-Marcan. It appears in Mark unharmonized, in a multiplicity of variations, so could scarcely be the work of an individual. The same conclusion seems to emerge when the contents are considered:

> How would Mark come to introduce such an idea into a tradition that knew nothing of it? There is no discernible reason for his doing so. Historically speaking, the idea cannot be fully understood just from Mark directly. We find it there ready-made, and Mark is under its sway, so that we cannot even speak of a *Tendenz* (Wrede, 1971, 145).

The problem for Wrede is thus basically one of tradition-history: what gave rise to the concept of the messianic secret?

Wrede's answer starts with the obvious importance which the resurrection had for the community's faith: belief in the messiahship of Jesus as the future Judge of the world dates from this point. The idea does not necessarily presuppose that the life of Jesus was messianic; but secret messiahship does presuppose a belief in the

* First published in *SE* 3, TU 88 (1964) 87–104. Translated by C. M. Tuckett.

future Messiah. How could the theory have arisen "if everyone already knew and reported that Jesus had openly given himself out as messiah on earth . . . What would have prompted making the messiahship of Jesus a matter of secrecy in contradiction to the original idea, in other words simply denying in retrospect Jesus' messianic claims on earth" (227)? There is scarcely any other possibility than "that the idea of the secret arose at a time when as yet there was no knowledge of any messianic claim on the part of Jesus; which is as much as to say at a time when the resurrection was regarded as the beginning of the messiahship" (228). The original idea must have already been losing ground, and already in the life of Jesus "hints about his future standing, characteristics and utterances were being found" (ibid.). So, as a consequence of resurrection faith, messiahship was read back into the life of Jesus. The messianic secret is thus "a transitional idea and it can be characterised as the after-effect of the view that the resurrection is the beginning of the messiahship at a time when the life of Jesus was already being filled materially with messianic content" (229). This has implications for the historical life of Jesus: for the secrecy idea could only have arisen at a time when nothing was known of any messianic claim by Jesus. This therefore seems to be a positive indication "that Jesus actually did not give himself out as messiah" (230).

Although not central to the whole study, this final claim provoked critical reaction which almost universally took the form of vehement rejection of Wrede's theory. The result was that the starting-point which had been carefully established, i.e. the consideration of the problem of the tradition–history involved, remained virtually ignored. It was only with the work of the form critics that this aspect of Wrede's work was taken up again and used to clarify the presynoptic material in the tradition. Thus R. Bultmann, in *The History of the Synoptic Tradition*, took up again the question of the tradition–history of the messianic secrecy concept, though in another connection. On the basis of form-critical analysis, he came to the conclusion, in contrast to Wrede, that the elements which make up the messianic secret all occur in Mark's redactional material. But he thought that in other respects Wrede's proposed solution could be maintained. Thus for Bultmann too, the theory of the messianic secret was "a veiling of the fact that faith in Jesus' Messiahship begins from belief in his resurrection".[2] Bultmann's literary–critical analysis is, in my view, convincing; but his interpretation of the secrecy theory is open to question. Is it possible to retain Wrede's explanation of the tradition–history involved when its basis, i.e. the pre-Marcan origin of the secrecy theory, is rejected? Can it be shown that the evangelist consciously adapted a tradition which presented the life of Jesus as unmessianic? In what follows, the sayings about the secrecy concept will be briefly examined first with this in mind. Part two will consider the origin of the secrecy motif in the history of the tradition; and in part three, the interpretation of the secret in the context of Mark's Gospel will be discussed.

## I

As far as Jesus' secrecy commands are concerned, there is no question that the exorcisms reported in the summary sections are secondary, i.e. they have been formulated by the redactor. These commands of Jesus to the demons to be silent (1:34; 3:11f) stem from the evangelist. The pre-Marcan pericope 1:21–8 is different. Here the command to silence is connected with the exorcism. It is thus an original part of the story. However, this proves nothing about a pre-Marcan origin of the secrecy theory, for, as Bultmann has shown, recognition by the demons and commands to silence are a part of exorcism stories in general.[3] But Mark himself will have understood it in terms of the theory of the messianic secret.

The redactor's hand can easily be traced in the way that other miracle stories are presented. Their statements about secret messiahship can be removed as secondary without disrupting their logic. Where these statements are part of the pre-Marcan tradition (e.g. the withdrawal from the crowds in 5:40, or the separation of the patient in 8:23), they have parallels in secular miracle stories.[4] This has been established in detail by Bultmann. But this means that the evangelist's tradition was already completely coloured by the belief that the earthly Jesus was the Messiah; for if the exorcism in 1:21–8, with its demon's confession, comes from the pre-Marcan tradition, the community prior to Mark which preserved this tradition about Jesus is unlikely to have understood the cry *ho hagios tou theou* ("the holy one of God") (1:24) in an unmessianic way. The same applies in the other miracle stories. The cultic worship of the *Kyrios* has affected the words and actions of those seeking help no less than the way in which the majesty of the miracle-worker himself is presented. There are thus no grounds for concluding that the evangelist knew of any discrepancy between messianic and unmessianic traditions about Jesus. This is confirmed by the fact that Mark's tradition already contained stories of confession and revelation, e.g. Peter's confession (8:27b–29) and the appended passion prediction (8:31), as well as the transfiguration story (9:2–8). The evangelist incorporated these elements into his theory of secret epiphanies by adding secondary commands to silence (8:30; 9:9–10).

The second basic motif of the secrecy concept, i.e. the lack of understanding by the disciples, can be seen more frequently in the pre-Marcan tradition.[5] Originally, it was perhaps simply a typically human reaction to divine revelation.[6] The evangelist not only repeats the motif, but also inserts it into his source (e.g. 14:40b) and independently creates it (9:10 and elsewhere), which indicates a change of meaning at the level of Mark's redaction: for it occurs explicitly in connection with the idea of Jesus' secret messiahship, when it refers back to some esoteric instruction (e.g. at the end of the transfiguration story) or when it points forward, as in other instances. It follows that the motif of lack of understanding, like the secrecy commands, presupposes an epiphany. The basis for Mark's redactional work is thus not the tradition of an unmessianic life of Jesus. Rather it is the idea, already present in the tradition, of the messiahship of the earthly Jesus.

Finally in this connection, there is the peculiar and often overlooked motif of the topological statements. Their significance can be made clear from the example of *ploiarion* ("little boat") or *ploion* ("ship"). The idea comes from the pre-Marcan tradition (1:19f; 4:36ff; 6:47ff) and is sometimes used quite generally (5:2ff; 6:53f; 8:10). But in Mark's redactional material it has special significance. It is used in contexts which show that the disciples, in contrast to the crowds, are especially close to Jesus. Mark has the *ochlos* ("crowd") remain behind on the sea-shore, while the Messiah reveals himself *en tǭ ploiǭ* ("in the boat") to his trusted friends by means of a miracle (4:36ff) or teaching (8:14ff). But this means that, in the redactional context of the secrecy theory, the motif signifies the place where revelatory events occur in secret.

Topological expressions have far more importance within Mark's redaction than can be dealt with here. But the idea of the *oikos* ("house") must be mentioned. It is not geographically fixed, and it appears where the revelation needs its own space, separate from the crowds.[7] The "mountain", to which Jesus withdraws either alone or with his disciples, is another example. There is too the typically Marcan *en tę̄ hodǭ* ("in the way"), as well the term *topos erēmos* ("desert place"): the latter is the place where Jesus prays and to which he retreats, and is thus again characteristic of the desire for concealment. All these are similar expressions which, insofar as they occur originally within the context of the secrecy theory, come from the redactor.

Though not part of the spatial background, what Mark says about those who accompany Jesus also has topological significance. The constant companions of Jesus are the "twelve", and it is they who first receive the revelations of the Messiah. The number can be varied. Sometimes only the four disciples who were called at the Sea of Galilee are mentioned. The motif comes from the call pericope (1:16–20), and Mark can use it, for example, in the introduction to Jesus' apocalyptic discourse (13:3). It is only in redactional material that the three disciples Peter, James and John are mentioned; these act as witnesses to characteristic manifestations of the revealer. Here, therefore, revelations take place amongst a narrower circle of the disciples. On the other hand, it almost seems to contradict this when, in the passage about the interpretation of the parables at 4:10, we hear of *hoi peri auton* ("those who were around him") as well as the twelve; and they, like the disciples, appear to have been granted the "secret of the Kingdom of God". Similarly, in the pericope about the relatives of Jesus, even the *ochlos* ("crowd") are said to be Jesus' confidants. However, the number of Jesus' disciples makes no material difference, and in the texts just mentioned the principle of secret epiphanies is not broken either. What really matters is the context of what is said, and this is quite clear in each instance: the wider circle of the disciples is set over against those who "stand outside". This means that the topological idea is not bound to any one expression of it; even the *ochlos* ("crowd") can be included in the inner circle if the situation demands it. All that matters is that the idea of messianic hiddenness, that any revelatory event occurs in isolation, is maintained.

We can now summarize what has been established so far and what follows from it:

1 The motif of the messianic secret appears very frequently in a variety of ways. This indicates that we should acknowledge the fundamental significance of the motif for the interpretation of the whole Gospel.
2 Bultmann's analysis has been confirmed. The motif is basically redactional.
3 We have seen that the pre-Marcan tradition was itself already christologically coloured. Since this can be shown to be the case in individual pericopes, there is no need to prove that Mark has not used an unmessianic Jesus–tradition; Mark uses the traditions

of the community which have all been coloured by the community's confession of faith.

This means that the attempt to apply Wrede's history of traditions explanation of the secrecy concept to Mark's redactional work (as is still done by Bultmann) must be dropped. Since Mark probably did not know any unmessianic traditions about Jesus, his use of the secrecy theory cannot be seen as an attempt to reconcile messianic and unmessianic traditions about Jesus. (A corollary of this is that the Marcan secrecy motif cannot be used as even an indirect argument against the historical Jesus' having a messianic self-consciousness.)

Whether Wrede's view can be maintained at the level of the pre-Marcan tradition, i.e. whether the secrecy idea in the pre-Marcan tradition presupposes the coming together of messianic and unmessianic traditions about Jesus, is another matter. This raises the question of the origin and tradition history of the motif in Mark's Gospel.

## II

The essence of the messianic secrecy motif is the paradoxical unity of hiddenness and revelation. Even though the hiddenness is not infrequently ruptured, e.g. when the commands to silence are disobeyed, the stress at the level of Mark's redaction still lies on the motif of hiddenness. This is clear (i) from the importance of the epiphany of the *Kyrios* in the pre-Marcan tradition; and (ii) above all from our conclusion that the lack of understanding and the commands to silence are redactional motifs.

The revealer's intention to remain hidden is also part of the redactional motif of hiddenness, as is the limitation of this hiddenness to a given time limit, i.e. Jesus' resurrection. (This anticipates what will be said about 9:9 later.)

This provides the starting-point for asking about the origin and tradition history of the motif in Mark's Gospel. There is no need here to go any further into the question of the universal correspondence between revelation and hiddenness, which is widespread both inside and outside the NT (e.g. Matt. 11:25ff; 28:17; Jewish wisdom teaching, etc.): it is a motif which is widely linked with the idea of revelation, but it does not clarify the special characteristics of Mark's messianic secrecy theory.

More important is the recent hypothesis that the messianic secret in Mark might derive from the christological tradition of gentile

Christianity, namely the tradition found in Phil. 2:6ff. According to this view, the messianic secret in Mark is modelled on the pattern of the gnostic myth, with its ideas of the cosmic descent of the pre-existent redeemer, his earthly presence in hidden form under the powers of the world, and his final exaltation to be the Cosmocrator.[8] This kind of derivation might explain the hiddenness motif in the messianic secrecy concept. However, a comparison between the "gnostic", or "pre-gnostic", redeemer myth and Mark's Christology shows that in other respects there are important differences. There is no "descent" idea in Mark's Gospel; that alone makes it unlikely that Mark's Christology includes the idea of pre-existence; this idea can scarcely be deduced from the fact that the verb *apostellein* ("send") is applied to the "Son", nor from the fact that Jesus' baptism is presented as an epiphany. Epiphany and adoption are not mutually exclusive; Jesus' baptism is understood as his adoption to be *huios tou theou* ("Son of God"), as can probably be deduced from the words of address in Mark 1:11 when compared with the parallel versions, and above all from the different form of expression used in Mark 9:7.[9] But it is not only this which tells against the connection with gnostic ideas. It is also notable that Mark's Gospel lacks any cosmological ideas which might be compared to the gnostic myth; above all, the intention of the revealer to remain hidden does not correspond with any parallel idea in genuine gnostic thought, where the hiddenness motif is connected more with what happens in the myth itself.

The result of all this is that Mark's motif of the messianic secret is not prefigured by the christological ideas found in Philippians 2; and we shall have to go further and reject even the possibility of any such genetic derivation, even in the sense of individual details being taken over from this idea.

W. Wrede gave other reasons for his view that the motif of the messianic secret was a pre-Marcan idea. He supported it by parallel texts in the Gospel of John. The relevant evidence can be divided into three groups:

1 Sayings about the Spirit, or Paraclete (e.g. 7:39; 14:19f, 26; 15:26f; 16:7, 12ff; 20:22). Here the revealer promises to his own followers perfect instruction through the Spirit who will be sent by the Father. There is a close relationship to what is said in Mark, in that the resurrection (or exaltation) of Jesus seems to be a temporal turning-point, and that a time of perfect revelation appears to follow a time when illumination is lacking. But it is clear that in John's understanding, the eschatological gift of salvation has

already been fully given with the arrival of the Son (11:24ff; 4.23f; 6:63). This means that the parallelism between John and the Marcan secrecy concept disappears. Certainly one could enquire whether the pre-Johannine tradition distinguished between a time of more limited illumination and a future time of complete instruction. The question can be focused on the problem of the Paraclete in the pre-Johannine tradition. But there is no need to show in detail that the points of contact with the Marcan secrecy motif would then be minimal.

2 A second group contains sayings about parabolic speech (10:6; 16:25, 29); these speak of failure to understand speaking in parables, which brings to mind the parallels in Mark 4:10ff and 7:17. This comparison shows that both the pre-Marcan and pre-Johannine traditions already presuppose a connection between speaking in parables and the motif of the failure to understand. The idea that the parables are incomprehensible may be suggested by the Hebrew term *mašal* (see R. Otto, J. Jeremias); it is also tied up with the fact that the community added secondary interpretations to parables which were in the tradition. But this then means that this idea was originally linked with speaking in parables, and not with a messianic secrecy motif. It is probably Mark who took the motif of the lack of understanding from the context of parabolic discourse and incorporated it into the wider context of the messianic secret. This is supported by the motif of lack of understanding being interpreted differently in John's Gospel. (See 16:25, 29: the dialectic of revelatory discourse involves hiddenness and frankness.)

3 Thirdly, and finally, there are the sayings about the disciples' insufficient understanding of Scripture, and these include a reference to the resurrection as the moment when more complete knowledge will ensue (2:22; 12:16; 20:9). In Mark one is reminded, as in the first group of sayings, of the mention of a point in time when misunderstanding will be removed. However, the differences should not be overlooked. Mark does not relate the misunderstanding of the disciples to any failure in their understanding of Scripture. Conversely, in the examples given from John's Gospel there is no intentionality involved. It is also striking that, in the context of John's Gospel, these sayings express an undialectical understanding of time, in that they appear to be wholly related to the future. Further, the idea of referring to Scripture, and also the fact that in John 2:22 the word of the Lord is set on a par with Scripture, support Bultmann's analysis which ascribed these texts to a post-Johannine ecclesiastical redactor. This can also be argued from a literary-critical point of view: all three passages can be removed from their context without disruption.

The result of all this is that, although John's Gospel may contain individual motifs which are reminiscent of the Marcan messianic secret, these statements are quite varied both in content and tradition–history. This excludes any theory which would derive the motif in question in Mark in this way. A messianic secrecy motif comparable to what we have in Mark is thus to be seen neither in the NT (nor in the traditions within the NT) nor in the contemporary environment. Wrede's attempt to explain the messianic secrecy theory in terms of its tradition–history is probably redundant. Of course, this is not to deny the fact that in shaping the motif, Mark used traditions which were already present. But this applies only to individual elements. It is only in the context of Mark's final redaction that they are linked together to form the comprehensive statement of the messianic secret.

## III

Mark writes as a member of his community. Mark's redactional messianic secret must therefore be seen in connection with the kerygma of the evangelist's community, as H. J. Ebeling stressed in his monograph,[10] and as Willi Marxsen subsequently spelled out in his article "Redaktionsgeschichtliche Erklärung der sogenannte Parabeltheorie des Markus".[11] The question arises, however, whether this so-called kerygmatic intention alone determines the gospel, or whether the concept of the messianic secret itself might not disclose a specific understanding of the gospel. We shall try to consider this question on the basis of individual sayings.

Mark 9:9 is part of the conversation which takes place on the way down from the mountain of the transfiguration. Its language and content indicate that, together with v. 10, it is a redactional construction, and in the wider context, it bears all the marks of the messianic secrecy concept. The selection of the three trusted disciples in v. 2 means that the transfiguration is already characterized as an esoteric revelation; the command for silence in our verse, and the typical misunderstanding of the disciples in v. 10, correspond to this. These statements can first be interpreted as direct address to the community – as different ways of referring to the "lofty nature of the divine mystery, which is here revealed to the reader [!]" (Ebeling, 200). But it is difficult to interpret the limitation of the silence command "until the Son of Man is risen from the dead" in the same way; for this appears to be fixing a definite point in time, and is thus directly opposed to a contemporary interpretation which is not bound by time.

Ebeling of course thinks that he can establish the directly kerygmatic reference here: he sees the transfiguration story as a preview of the resurrection, and he refers to parallels in apocalyptic literature. Here, the apocalyptic writer is instructed to keep the revelation which he has received secret, because it applies to later times (Dan. 8:26; 12:4, 9; As. Mos. 10:11f, and elsewhere). As in those texts, the command here too "indicates correspondingly the mysterious, i.e. revelatory, nature of what has happened" (Ebeling, 201). "As in the parallels which have been referred to, the given revelation points to the future, and its fulfilment is now to be awaited. This will confirm what the revelation, given here in advance, has already made certain to the witnesses in the present" (203). However, the interpretation of the transfiguration story as a preview of the resurrection is disputed, so the parallels drawn from the apocalyptic predictions are not necessarily convincing. But quite apart from this, we must note that the apocalyptic command to silence with a time limit aims to include the reader within the time of the keeping of the secret. The fact that the secret revelation has been partly realized then serves to guarantee the reliability of what has been predicted but has not yet happened. For Mark by contrast, the resurrection is an event lying in the past; it is this which is referred to here, without any parallel idea of a prophecy which has not yet been fulfilled. Thus, for this reason too, what is said in v. 9 cannot be taken as just a stylistic device, intended simply to stress the esoteric nature of what has been proclaimed.

Wrede showed that this passage has fundamental significance for the whole idea of the messianic secret. It is unlikely that the silence command refers only to the transfiguration and not to the messiahship of Jesus in general.[12] For, on the one hand, the transfiguration clearly belongs for the evangelist within the context of the messianic revelations of the earthly Jesus; and on the other hand, the command for secrecy is parallel to the other expressions of the messianic secret. These together constitute a unity which runs through the whole Gospel and forms a counterpart to the revelation given. But if then there is a material connection with the other secrecy elements, then the time limit in 9:9 cannot be taken in isolation; rather, it concerns the whole secrecy motif. It points forward to the resurrection as the time when the keeping of the secret, and that means the hiddenness of the Messiah, will come to an end.

The parable about the lamp and the lampstand and the appended sayings in Mark 4:21–3 are of pre-Marcan origin. This is shown by their presence in the sayings tradition, seen in the synoptic parallels. These sayings have been introduced into their present context by the evangelist. This can be seen from the Marcan introductory formula *kai elegen autois* ("and he said to them") (v. 21).[13] The significance of this for Mark's redaction was already stated by Wrede: if Mark introduces sayings material at this point, he does not do so "with some degree of embarrassment or by laboriously holding discrete ideas together, as if impelled not to permit such *logia* to perish, but in order to express an idea which is important in the context" (Wrede, 1971, 70f).

The original significance of the verses within the Jesus-tradition probably lies in the stress on the openness involved in the commission which Jesus claimed for himself and his preaching.[14] However, the specifically Marcan interpretation can only be discovered by considering the context. The natural starting-point for the interpretation seems to lie in the explanation of the parable of the sower which comes just before (vv. 13–20), as Ebeling thought.[15] These verses are then a paraenetical addition, saying that faith should not remain hidden but should lead to action. The contemporary application of this interpretation is obvious: as Ebeling says, it is aimed directly at the reader of the Gospel – it is a "direct application to the heart and mind of the community" (192).

But there are problems about this. The preceding verses comprise an original piece of source material containing the parable of the sower and its explanation; apart from our text, the evangelist added vv. 10–12 as well as the introduction (v. 1) and the conclusion (v. 34). But if it is a matter of a whole thematic unit, then it seems more correct methodologically to consider the redactional additions as a whole. This means that we should not interpret our text on the basis of the fact that it is appended to the immediately preceding explanation of the parable of the sower; rather, it should be interpreted in the context of the evangelist's theory about parables and in the light of the other redactional additions, especially as these statements correspond to one another; for here, as there, there is an echo of the same motif of "hiddenness and revelation".

In this connection we must consider the question of the meaning of the parables in 4:10. Here, in the double reference to the audience, the concept of the "twelve" is Mark's interpretative addition to the original *hoi peri auton* ("those around him"). The term *dōdeka* ("twelve") appears elsewhere in redactional contexts, including secrecy contexts where it has topological significance. It describes the smaller circle of people amongst whom revelation takes place. As we saw, this circle varies in size, i.e. even the traditional *hoi peri auton* is to be understood in a topological sense. But if the whole reference to the audience in v. 10 is part of the secrecy theory, this does not exclude a historical intention. For the topological expressions can clearly be used also as a stylistic means of presenting revelation as an event which, from the point of view of the author, lies in the past. This can be taken as certain, for the motif of the "twelve" refers back to the time of Jesus.

The interpretation of vv. 21–3 is also determined by this. These verses are joined to the explanation of the parables without any transition, and are thus addressed to the same "inner circle".[16] This means that here too the reference is not to the evangelist's community but to the time of Jesus. This shows that Wrede's interpretation of this text was right when he connected it with the idea of the messianic secret: as is explicitly said in 9:9, so too here, the secret revelation is limited in time. What is revealed to the disciples secretly in the time of Jesus is to be proclaimed openly in the future. We may therefore presuppose the same time-limit as in 9:9: after the resurrection what is hidden may be uncovered. Mark has "seen the resurrection as the dividing-line between two periods"[17] and from this he has developed the concept of the messianic secret.

Finally there are the three passion predictions of Jesus handed down by Mark. Linguistic considerations suggest that the last two predictions (9:30–2; 10:32–4) stem from the evangelist.[18] Further, it is unlikely that they were ever handed on in isolation, i.e. as original doublets of Jesus' first passion prediction in 8:31. For they are not complete units, but can only be understood in the total context of the Gospel. Their origin can be explained by the influence of the corresponding events of the passion narrative on the first passion prediction. 8:31 is different. Linguistic details suggest a pre-Marcan origin. The link with Peter's confession becomes clearer when one removes the command to silence (8:30) and v. 32a as Mark's interpretative additions. V. 31 could then have been handed down in the pre-synoptic tradition as a correction of Peter's confession by Jesus. It could have arisen on the basis of the community's faith in Jesus crucified and risen, confirming with a saying of Jesus the Church's Christology which differed from traditional Jewish ideas.

The relationship of this to the messianic secret has hardly ever been noted before,[19] although even a schematic comparison shows how very striking it is. Corresponding to each other are:

the *revelation motif* in the main part of the passion prediction (8:31; 9:31; 10:33f);
the *secrecy motif* in 8:30 (the command), 9:30 (Jesus' attempt to remain hidden), and in 10:32 (the separation of the twelve);
the *misunderstanding motif* in 8:32b (Peter's remonstration), 9:32 (the disciples' lack of understanding) and 10:35ff (the pericope about the request of the sons of Zebedee which has been added here redactionally).

We should therefore count the passion predictions as expressions of the messianic secrecy theory. Corresponding to the revelation of the suffering Messiah, whose majesty comes to expression in the predictions,[20] there is the failure of the disciples to understand and, above all, the hiddenness motif.

Linking the passion predictions with the other parts of the secrecy concept has various consequences. Since the passsion predictions point forward to a specific point in time, i.e. Jesus' death and resurrection, they have validity prior to this, but after their fulfilment they have only historical significance. The hiddenness remains until the fulfilment; but after this it comes to an end, the disciples understand, and open proclamation of Jesus' messiahship is permitted. If the passion predictions are incorporated within the whole pattern of the secrecy concept, this also has implications the other way: the time limit involved in them must be applied to the messianic secret in general. They stand on a par with the texts considered above (4:21f; 9:9f), and together with these, they qualify the Marcan secrecy motif as being something which is limited in time and belongs to past history. As such, it has validity only for the life of Jesus.

What we have tried to show about the concept of the messianic secret from these parts of the data can be confirmed by looking at Mark's redactional work as a whole. Although Mark's Gospel contains a large number of varied, even contradictory, statements, there is no doubt that on the whole the story constitutes a unity with its own temporal order, stretching from the appearance of the Baptist through to the death and resurrection of Jesus. Its contents correspond to this. For even if the author can hardly be credited with a systematic organization, or even any development in his portrayal of Jesus or the twelve, nevertheless the geographical notes show that the story goes along a certain path. After the introduction, the section about Jesus' activity begins in Galilee. This contains a few stories which were located in Galilee in the pre-Marcan tradition, but most of the units included here were not geographically fixed. The setting in Galilee, or its immediate neighbourhood, is maintained until the journey up to Jerusalem, which is indicated by 10:1, the start of the journey from Galilee to Perea. This direction of the Gospel is underlined by the three-fold passion prediction which begins after Peter's confession.

The numerous spatial and temporal links, which Bultmann showed to be part of the redactional material in the second Gospel,[21] have material significance in this context too. Connecting links made by verbs (*exelthein* ("to come out") etc.), the use of adverbs of place (e.g. *ekeithen* ("from there") in 6:1; 7:34 and elsewhere), and the specific redactional comments about the starting-point or goal of Jesus' journey are all characteristic of this. Even the topological expressions such as *oikos* ("house"), *oros* ("mountain"), *hodos* ("way"), *topos erēmos* ("desert place") belong here; despite their dogmatic significance, it is not fortuitous that they are taken from a vocabulary describing place.

Time references indicate the same thing. Adverbs (*euthus* ("immediately"), *palin* ("again"), *tote* ("then") and others), temporal links like *en ekeinais tais hēmerais* ("in those days") etc. all enable us to recognize the linear form of the Gospel. Above all, there is the well-known way the redactor has developed the account of Jesus' final activity in Jerusalem chronologically.[22]

All this shows that Mark is seeking to write the life of Jesus as an event complete in itself. It is not a critical view of history, but it is a historical view, insofar as one can describe an awareness of the distinction between past and present, evident in Mark's chronological and geographical perspectives, as "historical" thought. Eschatological salvation is manifested in the temporal sequence of the life of Jesus. The evangelist makes no distinction: the salvation *event* is presented as salvation *history*.

On the one hand, these temporal aspects of the messianic secrecy theory confirm the basic understanding of the Gospel; on the other hand, the theory itself must be seen against this background. Mark brings out the temporal elements in the theory, and this means that it is influenced by the process in which the gospel tradition is historicized. It becomes an element in the presentation of the life of Jesus as an event of salvation history. So it is not a "historically subsidiary idea"[23] which can be dissolved by reference to the history of the tradition, but rather an essential expression of a theology of salvation history. Its goal is the time after the resurrection; it implies the christological recognition that the story of the earthly Jesus does not remain on its own but points to his enthronement as Lord. Ecclesiologically, this means that Mark's community possesses remarkable self-awareness: it engages in a preaching which was only possible in hidden form during the life of Jesus (4:21ff). But now there are no bounds: that preaching now takes place with no time limit, i.e. until the end of time, and with all people in view (13:10). Above all, however, is the fact that, unlike the "twelve", the post-Easter community understands Jesus' messiahship (in contrast to the lack of understanding shown at the transfiguration or the passion predictions); the concept of the messianic secret thus implicitly expresses the fact that the presuppositions for a genuinely Christian preaching only exist after Easter.

There are still questions to be answered, but that is in the nature of the case. Mark writes a life of Jesus, but does not tell of the period in time after the resurrection; and it is only from this stand-point, in a presentation expounding Mark's ecclesiology, that the solution of the messianic secret could have been made clearer.

In what has been said here, the one important thing noted was the historical aim of the concept. What has already been established in the case of the topological expressions applies to the paradox of the messianic secret *in toto*: it does not contradict the historical orientation, but it needed incorporating into the historicizing presentation of the life of Jesus. It has a kerygmatic character, because it is the expression of the evangelist who is writing as the representative of his community. This means that the kerygmatic aim does not in fact contradict the historicizing tendency: rather, as a kerygmatic expression the messianic secret is to be seen "historically". It is precisely this that characterizes the Gospel. It is not simply "preaching", nor even "preaching and story",[24] but "preaching as story".

## NOTES

1 Göttingen, 1901 (ET 1971; all quotations from this).

2 Bultmann, 1963, 347; also 1951, 32. For more on this, see 1963, 348.

3 Bultmann, 1963, 209 n.1, 223.

4 Ibid., 224.

5 8:32f; 9:5f; 14:37ff; (5:31).

6 Cf. Matt 28: 16ff; John 20:25.

7 See G. Strecker, *Der Weg der Gerechtigkeit. Untersuchungen zur Theologie des Matthäus* (Göttingen: Vandenhoek & Ruprecht, 1962) 95.

8 See Schreiber, 1961.

9 The derivation of the idea of pre-existence from Mark 12:1ff (Schreiber, 167) presupposes a corresponding interpretation of the baptism story.

10 Ebeling, 1939.

11 *ZTK* 52 (1955) 255ff.

12 So, for example, A. Hilgenfeld, "Der mysteriöse Marcus und der reactionäre Jacobus", *Zeitschrift für wissenschaftliche Theologie* 46 (1903) 10; Ebeling, 1939, 198 n. 3.

13 Marxsen (n. 11), 259; J. Jeremias, *The Parables of Jesus* (ET London: SCM/New York: Charles Scribner's Sons, 1963) 14.

14 Jeremias, 121; Percy, 1953, 284.

15 Ebeling, 191 and elsewhere; see also ibid., n. 1.

16 On the other hand, the crowds are thought of as present again in v. 26; this corresponds with the speaking in parables in v. 2, and also vv. 33f, where there is the distinction made between teaching in parables "to them" and explaining the parables "to the disciples".

17 Wrede, 1971, 72.

18 Despite what is said by H. E. Tödt, *The Son of Man in the Synoptic Tradition* (ET London: SCM/Philadelphia: Westminster, 1965) 172ff, 201f [Strecker argues this in detail in his article "The Passion- and Resurrection-predictions in Mark's Gospel", *Interpretation* 22 (1968) 421–43. (German *ZTK* 64 (1967) 16–39).]

19 See, however, Wrede, 1971, 82f (also the two-fold scheme on p. 101). It does not occur in Ebeling's division. For 9:30f, see Percy, 1953, 293.

20 Wrede, 1971, 84.

21 1963, 339f.

22 Bultmann, 1963, 341; Dibelius, 1934, 223.

23 See Marxsen (n. 11), 267 n. 2.

24 So G. Bornkamm, art. Evangelien, formgeschichtlich, *RGG*, 3rd edn, vol. ii, col. 750.

# 5

# *The Question of the Messianic Secret in Mark*[*1]

EDUARD SCHWEIZER

## I *Presuppositions*

As long ago as 1901 W. Wrede showed that the messianic secret is a redactional construction of Mark, and belongs to the history of dogma, not to the life of Jesus.[2] There is no going back on this insight. On the other hand, E. Sjöberg has correctly called attention to the fact that between the life of Jesus and Mark's redaction there lies a long tradition–history, which Wrede did not deny but which he nevertheless regarded in far too uniform a manner.[3] We must therefore first see which statements were already part of Mark's tradition. The fact that the demons recognize Jesus and are silenced was certainly part of the tradition;[4] so too were the healings in private,[5] and perhaps also the command to tell no one until after the healing had been ratified by the priests.[6] Further, it had no doubt already been said before Mark that parables need interpretation.[7] Sjöberg's most important reference is to Jewish apocalyptic and its influence upon the secrecy motif of 1 Cor. 2:6ff; Rom. 16:25ff; Col. 1:26f; 2:2f; Eph. 3:1ff; 1 Tim. 3:16.[8] This is in fact Mark's background, though he develops his own, essentially different, conception.

This material must be expanded above all by the Qumran writings,[9] where statements about the "secret", or "mystery", refer almost always to God.[10] In contrast to the NT passages mentioned above,[11] the word often occurs here in the plural, and thus denotes a whole series of separate (eschatological) mysteries. Parallel concepts are "miracle" (1QS 11:3f), "truth" (1QH 7:26f) and "holy plan" (1QS 11:18f).[12] In the end, only God himself can understand the depth of his mysteries (1QS 11:18–20; 1QH 10:2f; cf. 13:3f). If chosen men receive a share in them (1QpHab 7:5; 1QH 11:3f, 10; 12:11–13;

* First published in *ZNW* 56 (1965) 1–8. Translated by C. M. Tuckett.

cf. 1QS 9:18f), that is a miracle effected by God's revelation.[13]

The NT passages mentioned above differ from these above all in the fact that as early as 1 Cor. 2:6–16 the saving event of the crucifixion of Jesus is the one "mystery" in which everything is included.[14] One can even say that Christ himself is *the* "mystery" of God (Col. 1:26f; 2:2; 1 Tim. 3:16; cf. Col. 4:3; Eph. 3:4), though increasingly the place of the crucified Christ is taken by the triumphant Christ journeying through the world, and finally by the Church itself (see already Eph. 3:4–6, 10; 5:32).

## II *The Differences in Mark's Conception*

The first thing that strikes us is the terminology: *mystērion* occurs only in 4:11,[15] where, unlike the synoptic parallels, it is in the singular. It is thus understood as something single and all-embracing, and Mark, like Paul in 1 Cor. 2:6ff, probably understood it to mean the cross. Whether that is also true for the tradition is doubtful. Further, Mark 4:11 shares with the Jewish apocalyptic texts and their NT offshoots the idea that this mystery can only be given (*dedotai*) to the chosen ones (*hymīn*) by grace though God's miracle. There are chosen people to whom the mystery is revealed. This distinguishes them from the world for which it remains incomprehensible folly.

But it is precisely here that questions arise. It is true that Mark joins all the texts mentioned above in asserting the inaccessibility of God, aiming to maintain the deity of God. He knows, like the apocalyptic writers, that only God's own revelation can unveil his mystery to man. He therefore also shows what efforts Jesus must continually make in order to bring God's mystery to men, especially his disciples (4:34; 7:17–23; 8:15–21, 27–33; 9:30–2; 10:32–4; cf. 5:37; 9:2; 13:3f, etc.). But whilst on the one hand it is clear that God's revelation everywhere bursts through irresistibly in Jesus' miracles and in his authority,[16] it is on the other hand vital for Mark that the disciples, who have received special instruction, show themselves despite this to be just as blind as the world (6:6b—8:26, especially 6:52; 7:18; 8:17–21). This is also shown by the failure of the disciples after the "open" teaching of 8:31, 32a (8:33; 9:6, 10, 18, 28, 32, 34; 10:35–7, 41), culminating in their sleeping, their flight and the denial at the climax of the story of Jesus (14:37, 40, 50, 66ff). The fact that God is at no man's disposal is thus understood far more radically than in the parallels. Not even the initiated, the chosen ones, have God at their disposal. He is thus in his essence God *absconditus sub contrario* ("concealed under the opposite"), and this cannot be overcome simply by miraculous communication.[17] We shall have to ask whether the commands silencing the demons and those who have been healed, absent from both the Qumran texts and the NT parallels, are not also connected with this radicalizing of the theology. Above all, however, we must investigate how Mark solves the problem that God is radically incomprehensible, that men are radically blind, but that still the miracle of revelation occurs.

## III *The Theory of Parables*

3:23 is a skilful redactional insertion.[18] It makes Jesus' speaking in parables an answer to the blindness of his own family and of the official Jerusalem representatives. It is meant to lead to the acknowledging of Jesus' authority (3:24–30) and to becoming a member of the family of God which consists of those who listen to Jesus and do God's will (3:31–5). For this purpose Jesus calls everyone to him (3:23). 4:1f starts the big parable discourse with a note about the setting which corresponds precisely with the other instances where Jesus wants to address and reach everyone with his "teaching".[19] The boat serves to emphasize how large and pressing the crowd is. 4:21f shows, after the interpretation of the first representative parable, that the lamp belongs on the lampstand, not under the bushel or the bed, and that what is hidden should be revealed.[20] Granted, one must have ears to hear[21] – it always remains a matter of God's gift – nevertheless Jesus' parable discourse is a call to hear in this way, and is a promise for those who do hear.[22] The most important reference for Mark's own understanding is 4:33f, where he himself speaks most clearly.[23] Here the parable discourse is seen as the only possible means of communication appropriate for human beings. It is not meant to conceal; it aims to reveal and reach men. This certainly expressed the fundamental inaccessibility of God: *only* in a parable, only in a picture can we comprehend him at all, not in direct speech. Certainly this inaccessibility is even more underlined by the special instruction given to the disciples. But 4:33b shows that the parable discourse in itself is an attempt to bear witness to God before men in such a way that the one who is fundamentally inaccessible is revealed to them. This programme is simply carried out more consistently in the case of the disciples. It is thus clear from all these instances that the parable discourse is speech which is appropriate for revealing the incomprehensible mystery of God to human beings.

When we turn to 4:10–13, the question arises as to what is tradition and what redaction. It is certain that not only the parable but also its interpretation is pre-Marcan. It is also certain that v. 10 is a seam, in which the question about the parable told by Jesus has been reshaped into a fundamental question about parables in general, and where at the same time the twelve have been introduced.[24] Further, it is certain that behind v. 11f there lies a tradition, whatever its details may have been.[25] Has Mark inserted it here? This is not as certain as might at first sight appear. It is clear that it is a tradition which is relatively unusual in Mark and uses strange terminology. It goes back to an Aramaic basis, perhaps to an Isaiah Targum, and occurs in the community's tradition outside Mark (John 12:40; Acts 28:26f), where it explains the unbelief of the world. It is probable that v. 10 (with the singular *parabolē* and without *syn tois dōdeka*) together with v. 13a constituted the pre-Marcan transition from parable to interpretation, and that this was transformed at a later stage of the tradition by the introduction of v. 11f. But who was responsible for this?

Now we can see the shift from this one parable and its interpretation to a fundamental statement about parables (in the plural) not only in the change assumed in v. 10, but also in the step from v. 13a to v. 13b. Thus at two different places and in two different ways, we find this advance to a statement of principle. They cannot both stem from the same author. But v. 13b is unlikely to have existed at the stage of the tradition where parable and interpretation were linked, i.e. before the inclusion of v. 11f. The picture of Jesus as sighing, and generally expecting no understanding of his parables, scarcely fits with the tendency to make everything clear through a precise interpretation of all the details. But this corresponds precisely with Mark's theology.[26] Even the disciples show themselves to be blind. Because of their lack of understanding, Jesus' wish to reveal is in danger of being frustrated. They are separated from the crowds at best by Jesus' special loving care for them, not by any better understanding on their part. The real elucidation of the parable discourse (8:32a as opposed to 4:33a) follows at 8:31, and even this the disciples do not understand at all (8:33). 4:11 sees things quite differently. Here those "inside" are sharply distinguished from those "outside". Here there is a group of chosen ones, for whom the mystery is no longer incomprehensible and to whom the mystery has been "given", whereas in 4:13b a fundamental blindness with regard to all parables is made clear from the case of this one parable. In 4:11f there is the secrecy idea of Qumran and the other NT passages mentioned above; what is said here is thus also reminiscent of predestination. It all stands much closer theologically to the community which attached the interpretation in 4:14ff and thereby described itself as the possessor of the key to the mystery. But for Mark all, if one can put it this way, are predestined to blindness, and all are called to perception. This is most clearly visible at 8:14 where a very similar prophetic saying is applied not to those "outside" but specifically to the disciples, and where the following story (8:22–6), with its continuation in vv. 27ff and vv. 34ff, shows that only God's miracle can open blind eyes, but that God wishes to perform this miracle.

The expression *en parabolais* is certainly part of the pre-Marcan tradition; the word was probably therefore already connected with the parable tradition prior to Mark. Equally certainly, the interpretation was added to the parable of the sower prior to Mark. It was thus already asserted that a parable without interpretation remains hidden, and that the special teaching which interprets it has been given not to the world, but only to the Church, where the parable is correctly applied to the word of preaching. It is therefore probable that 4:11f had already been placed between the parable and interpretation in the pre-Marcan tradition. The community had thus adopted the Isaiah quotation as in John 12:40 and Acts 28:26f to describe the unbelieving world from whom the following interpretation remained hidden.[27] The first step in the tradition was thus the addition of the interpretation with the original form of v. 10 and perhaps v. 13a; the second step transformed v. 10 and added v. 11f; finally, Mark was able to take over the idea of the special concern of Jesus for the twelve (v. 11a) together with a provisional distinction between them and the people (v. 11b). But at the same time, in a third step, he used v. 13b to establish that in the last resort the twelve also belong to the blind world. He thus points forward to 8:17ff.[28]

## IV *Mark's Answer*

The first half of the Gospel shows the blindness of the Pharisees (3:6 as the conclusion of the first section), of Jesus' own fellow-citizens (6:1–4 as the conclusion of the second section) and of the disciples (8:17–21 as the conclusion of the third section). Jesus then speaks in 8:31 for the first time without parables and openly (8:32 is parallel to 4:33) of the suffering of the Son of Man.[29] But even this plain speaking remains incomprehensible to the disciples (8:33). Thereafter, Jesus summons the whole crowd and challenges people to become disciples (8:34). This means therefore: 1. Only in discipleship, following in the way of the cross, can one understand Jesus' way to the cross and so Jesus himself.[30] 2. In discipleship the distinction between those "inside" and those "outside" disappears: all people are called to it, not only the twelve (8:34a). Both these points are confirmed in the following two passion predictions, where an immediate misunderstanding by the disciples and a call to discipleship are attached;[31] similarly, in 15:39 it is not a disciple but the gentile centurion who is the first to understand what has happened on the cross; and in 15:41 it is not the disciples who are mentioned, but the women, who will see the empty tomb first and who have followed Jesus and served him. Finally, in 16:7 a message will be sent by the angel to the disciples that Jesus will go before them into Galilee, as he was doing already on the way to the cross (10:32), and as he was to promise them in 14:28 in the midst of their failure.[32]

In Qumran the call to follow him in whom God's "mystery" is revealed is of course lacking. Neither are there any commands to silence there. The question arises of whether both these things belong together. Are not the commands to silence to be explained in that one cannot understand God's revelation in Jesus in any other way than in the way of discipleship, and so only after the suffering of the Son of Man? So it is indeed the messianic, rather than the unmessianic material which causes Mark trouble.[33] The juxtaposition of the *theios anēr* idea and that of the fundamental hiddenness of the revelation[34] are both pre-Marcan and cause difficulties. They are resolved by saying that God's revelation breaks through powerfully and irresistibly – thus the commands to silence are continually broken[35] – but that it is bound to be misunderstood except where the disciple learns the real secret, the suffering of the Son of Man, by following in this way of suffering.[36] But on this the following article (that of U. Luz) should be considered.[37]

## NOTES

1 This and the following essay come from my summer 1964 seminar on the topic. A whole series of students have therefore contributed to them. The two authors also have their own individual insights and misunderstandings as is shown by some, though not too important, differences between the view of my assistant, for whose help I am extremely grateful, and my own.

2 Wrede, 1971, 131.

3 Sjöberg, 1955, 150ff.

4 See Mark 4:39; Sjöberg, 150f, and Luz, p. 81 below. On the first motif, the texts cited in n. 36 below seem to me more relevant than the hellenistic ones.

5 See Luz, p. 77.

6 1:43f; Sjöberg, 158f.

7 Sjöberg, 166f; see n. 24.

8 Sjöberg, 1ff. On the other hand, the concept of the hidden Messiah plays no role (against Sjöberg, 125).

9 G. Bornkamm, art. "*mysterion*", *TDNT* iv, 815, 819.

10 I am grateful to Herr Wiard Popkes for the list of references.

11 But cf. Matt 13:11; Luke 8:10; 1 Cor. 4:1; 13:2; also the substance of Rom. 11:25; 1 Cor. 15:51.

12 This plan applies to all periods of time, but especially the End-time (1QpHab 7:7f, 12–14) and also the time of iniquity (1QS 4:18).

13 There is also talk of the mystery of wickedness (1QH 5:36; 1QM 14:9f; 1QXXVII 1:2). This is also to be understood in apocalyptic terms and remains subordinate to the divine plan.

14 Bornkamm, *TDNT* iv, 829; also E. Schweizer, art. "*pneuma*", *TDNT* vi, 425f and n. 617.

15 The same is true for other terms. The following are completely absent: *teleios* ("perfect") (1 Cor. 2:6; Col. 1:28), *apokryptein* ("to hide") (1 Cor. 2:7; Col. 1:26; cf. 2:2; Eph. 3:9), *apokalyptein* and *apokalypsis* ("to reveal" and "revelation") (1 Cor. 2:10; Rom. 16:25; Eph. 3:3, 5), *gnōrizein* ("to make known") (Rom. 16:26; Col. 1:27; cf. 2:2; Eph. 3:3, 5, 10). Other terms such as *sophia* ("wisdom") (1 Cor. 2:6; Col. 1:28; 2:3; Eph. 3:10; cf. Rom. 16:27), *phaneroun* ("to manifest") (Rom. 16:26; Col. 1:26; cf. 1 Tim. 3:16), *synesis* ("understanding") (Col. 2:2; Eph. 3:4), *geneai* ("generations") (Col. 1:26; Eph. 3:5) are not redactional and are used in a quite different connection (Mark 6:2; 4:22; 12:33; *genea* only in the singular).

16 See Luz, pp. 76–80.

17 I have wondered whether some polemic against Jewish Christianity can be seen here (so S. Sandmel, *Journal of Bible and Religion* 31 (1963) 294–300). But it seems to me very unlikely. Certainly Mark is very interested in the positive position of the Gentiles (F. Hahn, *Mission in the New Testament* [ET London: SCM, 1965], pp. 111ff; Schweizer, 1964a, 340, 352f; [cf. Schweizer, 1964b, 422, 429f]); but often it is clear that the real opponents are the Jewish authorities alone, i.e. the Pharisees and scribes, and not the Jewish people (see especially 3:6–8; 7:1ff/14; 10:1f; 11:18, 27/32; 12:12, 13, 18/37 [though cf. v. 34]; 14:1f; 15:11). It should rather be noted that Galilee is valued more highly than Jerusalem, and that, despite their denial of Jesus, the disciples who come from there (see also 15:41) are given the promise of an appearance of Jesus in Galilee (14:28; 16:7). For I am convinced (with U. Wilckens, *Der Ursprung der Überlieferung der Erscheinungen des Auferstandenen, Dogma und Denkstrukturen* [ed. W. Joest, W. Pannenberg, 1963], pp. 78ff, n. 60) that Mark's readers, who certainly knew of Easter appearances, must have interpreted 16:7 in this way, even if Mark did not (as I believe he did not) go on to record them after 16:8.

Is there here (as there probably is at Mark. 5:20) a tradition about the start of the mission outside Jerusalem? If so it contradicts the picture of Acts, where everything derives from the gift of the Spirit in Jerusalem. In this case there would possibly be some hidden polemic against a church that was based too much on Jerusalem, with Galilee in some way prefiguring gentile Christianity. However, quite apart from the question of whether Jerusalem played such a role, this is still unlikely in view of the positive way in which the *people* from Jerusalem are presented from 1:5 to 12:37b. *Barn.* 5:9 (cited by Wrede, 1971, 106) is thus not far wrong.

18 Schweizer, 1963, 97f; 1964a, 344f; [cf. 1964b, 425].

19 See 2:13; 6:33; Schweizer, 1963, 95f; 1964a, 340.

20 Naturally there is tradition here, as is shown by the agreement in terminology with the texts collected above (*phaneroun* ("to manifest"), *krypton* ("hidden"), *apokryphon* ("secret")). But it is presumably Mark who has introduced the sayings at this point.

21 Verse 23 takes up v. 9, and therefore shows that, as v. 21f implies, the parable is intended to be heard.

22 Whatever else the meaning of v. 24f may be, this much is clear. Probably vv. 24b, 25a promise that whoever now hears correctly will be given even more insight.

23 Schweizer, 1963, 98f, 100.

24 J. Jeremias, *The Parables of Jesus* (ET London: SCM; New York: Charles Scribner's Sons, 1963) p. 14.

25 Ibid., pp. 15ff.

26 See 7:17f, where the disciples ask about *tēn parabolēn* ("the parable") (!) and Jesus' reproach then follows.

27 However, if it is Mark who has placed the verses here, he has introduced them simply on the basis of link-words at the first place where there is mention of special instruction given with a parable. His own ideas follow in 4:13b and 8:17ff.

28 Ebeling, 1939, 147f, noted something very important when he saw that the primary mystery is the person of Jesus, whereas words which are not understood, but are made clear by interpretation, are only a mystery in a secondary sense. Mark is concerned with that "primary" mystery; but he refers it entirely to Jesus' way of the cross, not to the person of Jesus as in any way separate from this.

29 Wrede, 1971, 67ff, 215ff, confused the discussion in claiming, on the basis of 9:9, that the resurrection is decisive. The Christology of Rom. 1:4; Acts 2:36 (or rather 13:33) has nothing to do with the Marcan Christology. 9:9 is an isolated instance, determined by the relationship between transfiguration and resurrection, and even here it is linked with the suffering of the Son of Man (9:12). Similarly, 8:33, 34 only take up out of 8:31 the idea of suffering. Even the eschatological–apocalyptic sayings 8:38; 9:1 simply underline the importance of discipleship, following in the way of the cross.

30 Ebeling also points to the connection between announcements of suffering and paraenesis (p. 166f).

31 Schweizer, 1964a, 349f; [cf. 1964b, 428f]. Also 9:35–7; 10:43–5 are formulated quite generally (*hos an* ("whoever"), *anti pollōn* ("for many")); 9:38ff is directed against too narrow a view of the twelve; whether the *akolouthountes* ("those who follow") of 10:32 are limited to the twelve alone is at least uncertain; see too 13:37.

32 It is certainly doubtful if this means to "go at your head" (against J. Weiss, *Die Schriften des NT*[2] *ad loc.* (since the 2nd edn is missing in Zurich, I have cited it as in Taylor, 1952, *ad loc.*); see R. H. Lightfoot, *In memoriam E. Lohmeyer* (ed. W. Schmauch, 1951) 115. The present tense in 16:7 (whereas 14:28 has the future) counts against this suggestion. The verse is rather to be understood as in 6:45 (cf. Matt. 21:31 Q) in a more general way; but that does not alter the fact that Jesus shows the way in which the disciples are to follow.

33 Conzelmann, 1968, 42f; see Sjöberg, 1955, 115f, against Wrede, 1971, 217ff.

34 Schreiber, 1961, 157f. No doubt the miracle stories of the gospel tradition show the influence of hellenistic *theios anēr* ideas. After reading D. Georgi, *Die Gegner des Paulus im 2.Korintherbrief* (1964), especially pp. 282–92, I am inclined to agree with Luz (p. 89 here and n. 7) that these ideas have not only influenced a series of individual stories, as might be used in preaching, instruction or discussion, but that also, prior to Mark, one may imagine a more or less complete Christology of this kind. Mark starts from this, but he also distances himself from it with his stress on the theology of suffering.

35 Ebeling in particular, pp. 116ff, points to this; but see too Wrede, 1971, 128.

36 This explains the apparent contradiction between Mark 1:34 end; 3:11 and 1 Cor. 2:8. What the powers here too fail to understand is not Jesus' character as a *theios anēr*, but God's plan of salvation which is fulfilled on the cross. Their knowledge is thus that of Jas. 2:19b. See too 1 Pet. 1:12; on the other hand, the Qumran community shares with the heavenly powers in having insight into God's mysteries (1QH 3:19–23; 1QS 4:22).

37 Apart from details where I differ, I would ask whether one should not see the unity of the miracle–secret and the messianic secret as more tightly knit, though the suggestion that only the demons can engage in messianic preaching proper and hence that this should be clearly distinguished from the other healings, seems to me to be very fruitful for the discussion. But where Mark is writing freely (3:11f), the aim of the prohibition is materially the same as in the healings. For even the prohibition against spreading abroad the news of a miracle is still a ban on proclaiming Jesus' divine authority in the present in a way that would be misunderstood. 1:25 belongs to the tradition, and 1:34, connected to it, is expressed rather more cautiously than 3:12, but probably means the same. The difference lies in the fact that in the exorcism of 1:25, the miracle consists precisely of the silencing of the powerful demon, just as in the healings it is in the ending of the illness (see Luke 4:39, Jesus' *epitīmān* ("rebuke") against the fever, as in Mark 1:25 against the demon; Mark 4:39 has the stilling of the sea by Jesus' *epitīmān* and a "silence command" to the storm). Here a breaking of the command is impossible, because Jesus' power over the demons leads to their overthrow. Mark himself interpreted the command, as in the healings, as a ban on making the messianic secret known prematurely (1:34; 3:12). Finally I wonder, though without claiming any certainty, whether it is a coincidence that the three places

where a silence command is not disobeyed (3:11f; 5:43; 8:26?) occur at the transitions between sections 1 and 2, 2 and 3, and 3 and 4. These are followed, respectively, by the choice of the twelve, their sending out and their open special instruction – in the second case admittedly only after the rejection of Jesus (in Nazareth a silence command would naturally be impossible in view of 6:5f) though it has already happened elsewhere. Also the short note in 1:34 leads to the private discussion with the disciples and the reference to Jesus' commission to preach in 1:35–9.

6

# *The Secrecy Motif and the Marcan Christology**

ULRICH LUZ

The "messianic secret" is still a mystery. H. Conzelmann called it the "hermeneutical presupposition of the genre 'gospel'",[2] and thus in effect outlined a new "mystery": the question of the Christology which in Mark's day demanded both the messianic secret idea itself and its embodiment in a Gospel. Mark belonged to a hellenistic community which had taken over numerous traditions about Jesus Christ from the vicinity of Palestine: messianic miracles which were proclaimed, material used in polemic or belonging to catechetical tradition, mostly material that was significant for the life of the community, and a collection of oddly isolated eschatological material.[3] There was also the passion narrative which, separated the rest, was perhaps handed down complete as a memorial (anamnēsis) in worship.[4]

What was the relation of the passion narrative to the rest of the Christ tradition? Christ had been made manifest in his miracles, and the proclamation of him was based on miracle[5]; his power and authority for the present day were clear in the controversy dialogues. So what could the passion add to that? Did it not contradict the rest of the Christ proclamation and need to be superseded by the miracle of the resurrection? And how was the community's suffering,[6] which Mark understood differently from his tradition, related to the view of reality that lay behind the miracle stories? Miracle stories and passion narrative, the divine man (*theios anēr*) and the Crucified, needed relating in a new way. Mark's Gospel grew out of this situation.[7]

The secrecy motif is found in Mark's healing miracles, exorcisms and his accounts of Jesus instructing the disciples. Our method will be to consider these three groups separately, since it cannot be

* First published in *ZNW* 56 (1965) 9–30. Translated by R. Morgan.

assumed that the secrecy motif means the same thing in each case. We are really only concerned with the Marcan redaction, and will use form criticism and examine motifs and word statistics[8] in working out what is redactional material.

## I

First the healing miracles. The material seems to provide a variegated picture. Some pericopae lack the motif of keeping the healing secret, whereas others have an express command of Jesus to keep it secret, or at least an indication that might be understood in this sense. There is also great variety as regards the origins of the motif. Sometimes it is clearly there in the tradition; often it is Mark's editorial insertion. The data may be classified thus:

In a few cases, notably 2:1–12 and 3:1–6, there is no hint of a secrecy. This is no great problem because in both cases new meanings have in the course of time been superimposed upon the original aim of the stories. The miracle story in Mark 2:1–12 is now intended only to demonstrate the *exousia* ("authority") of the Son of Man to forgive sins. This aim is incompatible with secrecy. The healing on the sabbath of the man with the withered hand (3:1–6) requires an element of publicity for the sake of the controversy dialogue. Secrecy here would also make the redactional decision of the Pharisees and Herodians to kill Jesus (v. 6) hard to understand. In the case of the woman with a flow of blood (5:25–34) the large crowd is a prerequisite of the scene. The passage is only significant in that the connecting verse 24a, "a great multitude followed him", probably stems from Mark himself.[9] The healing miracle in the second main part of the Gospel (8:27–10:52) will be considered below.[10]

The Marcan summaries contain significant data. The passage 6:53–6 is probably entirely redactional, despite a few unmarcan words.[11] The healings take place in public, in villages, towns and country, at times in the market-place. The whole neighbourhood is present. The meaning of the scene is clear; it shows the extraordinary success of Jesus' healing activity and its enormous scope and impact. Jesus is the wonder-worker or thaumaturge; wherever he appears it is an event. A command to silence is not only absent; the whole design and meaning of the scene make it impossible. Jesus' success is neither evaluated nor interpreted here; the scene is simply intended to show how well known Jesus became through his public healing.

In the two other summaries (1:32–4; 3:7–12) the situation seems to be rather different on account of their silence commands. But that is only apparently the case. In both instances the command to silence is directed at the demons alone. This is "because they knew him" (1:34), or after they had recognized him as God's Son (3:11). However we are to interpret the silence commands, the roots of the conception are not to be found here in the healings. Taking on their own the parts of the summaries concerned with healings, the picture is in full agreement with 6:53–6: Because Jesus healed people, many flocked to him (1:33; 3:8). It is clear, especially in the second summary, that Mark's real aim is to describe Jesus' great impact, seen in the people flocking to him. The healings are only the occasion for that (3:10). 1:32ff is also concerned mainly with the people coming to him.[12] Jesus' work takes place in a house (Peter's) only on account of the preceding pericope (vv. 29–31). We should thus note that in both summaries, the healings and the exorcisms are treated differently. Only the latter come under the silence command. We shall have to keep this difference in mind. The aspect we consider here is the question – at present it is no more than a question – whether the secrecy motif in the miracle stories may not have had a different significance from the messianic secret in the exorcisms.

In a whole series of pericopae the setting of the miracle itself provides a degree of hiddenness.[13] Healings take place in a house (1:29–31; 2:1–12; 5:21–43; cf. 7:24–30), in the synagogue (3:1–6; cf. 1:21–8) or apart from the people (7:31–7).[14] In these cases Mark has normally taken the setting from the tradition. It corresponds to a generally observable tendency in miracle stories to have the actual miracle happening not in public view but in private, just as the actual miracle is not described but indicated only through its impact.[15] One must of course ask how far this traditional feature has significance for Mark in the context of his secrecy theory, all the more since it is elsewhere probable that Mark has made traditional motifs the occasion and starting-point for his secrecy theory.[16] But it is worth noting that the redactional interpretation of all these stories which did not basically take place in public, stresses the public significance of these miracles: 1:29–31 gives an opening for the summary which follows; the healing in 2:1–12 which in itself takes place in the presence of a large audience (2:4) is made the occasion for a disputation with the scribes, and following that the redactor has Jesus for the first time accompanied by "all the crowd" (2:13); the healing of the deaf-mute ends with the silence command being broken (7:36f). 7:24–30, which has the form of a healing rather than an exorcism[17] stresses in its redactional introduction that contrary to his wishes Jesus could not remain hidden (7:24). When 3:1–6 is made the occasion of the (redactional) decision by the Pharisees and Herodians to destroy Jesus, this can only be understood as a response to his public activity. Only 5:43 provides an exception to this rule.[18]

(8:22–6 is a special case. Jesus' command to the blind man, "Go not into the village", was very early on interpreted as a silence command,[19] but probably wrongly since the shorter text represented by B (Vaticanus) is probably the oldest. The question is whether the short command of Jesus is redactional. Vocabulary statistics cannot settle the issue. *Kōmē* ("village") (6:6, 56; 8:27) and *eiserchesthai* ("to enter") (1:21, 45; 2:1; 3:1; 7:17, 24) could well be redactional, whereas a prohibition beginning with *mēde* ("but not") would be odd. One should note that v. 26b refers back to v. 23a, a verse that is certainly traditional since both *epilambanesthai* ("to take hold") and *ekpherein* ("to carry out") occur only once in Mark. So 8:26b is also most likely to be tradition. But how did Mark understand this tradition? There are various reasons for supposing that he understood this pericope, unlike other stories of healings, symbolically. Just as 10:46–52 (the healing of the blind Bartimaeus, who becomes a follower of Jesus) is the close of the second main division, so this story (8:22–6) marks the end of the first. That other pericope is certainly to be understood symbolically.[20] Further, in 8:16 the disciples are reproached for their literal understanding of the feeding story, whereas 8:22–6 connects extremely well with the blindness of the disciples (8:18). So the story is probably not a miracle story but a symbolic presentation of the healing of humanity's blindness by Jesus.[21] Jesus' prohibition against entering the village is perhaps for Mark an indication of the significance of Jesus' saving action which draws the people to whom he grants sight out of their world. But this remains uncertain.)

We come now to the passages where Mark himself introduces a command to silence into a healing story.[22] Firstly, Mark 1:40–5. How much the evangelist himself has contributed to this story is disputed. Verse 45 certainly stems from Mark himself: *Kērussein* ("to proclaim"), *erēmos topos* ("desert place"), is clearly redactional material;[23] the adverbial *polla* ("much"), *exerchesthai* ("to come out"), *archesthai* ("to begin"), *ho logos* ("the word"), *hōste* with the infinitive ("so that"), *dynasthai* ("to be able"), *polis* ("city"), *eiserchesthai pros auton* ("to approach him") are at least frequently redactional.[24] The decision on what is tradition and what redaction is more difficult in vv. 43f. The vocabulary seems to belong to the tradition. This is the case with *embrimasthai* ("to be indignant"), *horān* ("to see"), *kai legei* ("and he says"),[25] and also of *ekballein* ("to cast out"), which is admittedly used frequently by the evangelist, but not with the meaning "to send someone away, dismiss".[26] Verse 44b may well belong to the tradition; it is quite unthinkable that Mark should have had a positive interest in the fulfilment of the OT purity laws. That leaves only the actual silence command in v. 44a which remains doubtful. *Horā* ("see") with the conjunctive is unusual in Mark, and so is the double negative,[27] whereas in the silence commands a preceding *mēdeis* ("nobody") is relatively frequent.[28] The total lack of explicit silence commands in the pre-Marcan tradition makes it at least possible that Mark himself formulated v. 44a redactionally. The parallel in the Egerton papyrus supports this.[29] Its meaning would then be interpreted through the tradition in which it is inserted, i.e. the healed man should be silent because it is Jesus' will that the representatives of official Judaism, the priests, learn of the healing so that in this way a *martyria* ("testimony") to Jews may be given. Be this as it may, it was at any rate Mark's intention to stress by v. 45 the quite different outcome of the scene: the healed man cannot contain himself but begins to proclaim. It is worth noting that Mark does not use some neutral word for the healed man's speaking, but the positive *kērussein* ("to proclaim"). *Ho logos* ("the word") is also a very positive expression, meaning the sum total of Christian proclamation; Mark takes the term over from the Church's tradition.[30] So according to Mark the miracle cannot remain secret, even when Jesus does not want it to be made known. By its very nature it breaks through the silence and leads into proclamation. This is to be seen primarily as Mark's positive message.

We turn now to the other passage which we still have to interpret: 7:36f. Verse 36 is certainly redactional, as is shown by the vocabulary *diastellesthai* ("to command") *mēdeni* ("to no one"), *hosos* ("whoever") *kērussein* ("the proclaim").[31] Verse 37 on the other hand is likely to stem from the tradition, since this probably contained the original "chorus conclusion"[32] of the healing miracle. The vocabulary also supports this view.[33] The parallelism with the passage considered earlier is striking. In both cases the event of the miracle is handed on by *kērussein* ("proclaiming"); so in both cases the breaking of the silence command is interpreted positively. The motif of the public success of this preaching, which we found at 1:45, is missing here because it was made superfluous by the tradition's chorus conclusion being used, and by 8:1. It is striking that the making public of the miracle is stressed precisely in gentile territory[34] (cf. earlier, at 7:24!). That may contain a conscious Marcan intention, like 15:39.

Looking back, the analysis of the three summaries 1:32ff, 3:7ff, and 6:53ff leads us to suppose that the silence command in the exorcisms and the silence motif in the healing narratives might be two fundamentally different things. We can now supplement this observation by another: these passages which we have discussed contain nothing about a "messianic secret". It is not the messiahship of Jesus, or his divine sonship which is to be kept secret but the event of healing, the miracle. It will therefore be better to call the secrecy motif in the healing narratives a "miracle secret".

A survey of all Mark's reports of healings showed that his interpretation of these pericopae is completely uniform,[35] regardless of whether or not they contained a silence command. In Mark's view the miracle is testimony intended for the public. Even where Jesus does not want this to happen it forces its way into the proclamation and is successful. So the silence just underlines this fact that the miracle cannot be kept hidden.[36] The miracle is evident in its own right. This interpretation was confirmed for us by the Marcan summaries.

There is now the question how this conception fits into the Christology of Mark; more specifically, how this type of silence command is related to the others.[37].

## II

The exorcisms which Mark includes in his Gospel give at first sight the same picture. Here, too, the miracle itself serves to make Jesus known in the whole region. The exorcism in 1:21–8 ends with a redactional note[38] that the news about Jesus spread through the whole region. In 5:19 the Gerasene demoniac is commissioned by Jesus to remain in his own territory and to tell his fellow-countrymen what a great thing God has done for him. Thus far the scene is certainly tradition, perhaps a founding legend of the church in the Decapolis.[39] But then it is probably Mark himself who goes further, consciously taking up and making minor corrections to what has preceded:[40] "And he went away and began to proclaim in the Decapolis[41] what Jesus[42] had done for him."[43] So here too we find again the same tendency of Mark which we found in the healing miracles, a tendency which there and elsewhere was accentuated by Jesus' silence commands and their being broken: miracles lead to the preaching of Jesus' power being extended; they proclaim it publicly and irresistibly.

There are, however, in the two Marcan summaries, silence

commands to demons. These clearly require a special interpretation, in particular because in contrast to the normal tendency, noted in the summaries and the two exorcisms mentioned above, to understand miracles as the occasion and empowering to preaching, these commands seem to stand on their own. So they must be interpreted as special cases and not too quickly harmonized with the silence commands discussed in the preceding section. The two passages are similar. In both cases the command is related to the person of Jesus: the demons are not to speak, because they know him (1:34b); they are not to reveal him after they have made him known as Son of God (3:11f). The differences between the two passages stem from the different contexts of the two summaries. The first puts the activity of Jesus more in the foreground whereas the second is mainly concerned with the reverence paid by the people and the demons; the exorcizing of the demons is totally absent in this case.

To interpret both these passages we must first ask what traditional motifs Mark might have used in forming his silence commands. We know from elsewhere of (a) the demon's address to the exorcist where the demon naturally recognizes the exorcist, even when the latter is a heavenly being.[44] Even closer linguistic parallels can be found in magical prayers.[45] (b) The command to the demon, "Be silent", is common,[46] but is always found in connection with the actual exorcism, as in Mark 1:25.[47] But this is at best an analogous motif to the silence command.[48]

This material shows that Jesus' being addressed by the demons in Mark is perfectly normal in exorcisms. The "confession" of the demons (1:24; 5:7; cf. 9:20)[49] turns out to be pre-Marcan, since it belongs to their nature for demons to be able to "sniff out" even a heavenly exorcist.[50] This is supported by the curious title *ho hagios tou theou* ("the holy one of God") at 1:24. One must consider carefully whether the Son of God title at 5:7 (cf. 3:11) is original or a Marcan replacement for an older title.[51]

But it is also apparent that Jesus' prohibition to the demons against making his nature known is without analogy in the tradition. This is where we must begin our interpretation. Why does Jesus lay this silence command upon the demons? The following possibilities require consideration:

(a) Because the demons are not the right proclaimers of Jesus' true nature. They recognize him to be unique, but are not appropriate proclaimers because although they are overpowered by Jesus, they are not his disciples.

(b) Because according to Mark Jesus did not yet wish to be revealed. The demons are silenced precisely because they alone are the ones who recognize Jesus' true nature. Why? Clearly because it is not now possible or not the right time to proclaim or understand Jesus as Son of God. In that case the prohibition to the demons must be interpreted as a pointer to understanding Mark's Christology.[52]

A further observation allows us to exclude the first possibility for the moment. Mark's making Jesus forbid the demons to proclaim him has nothing to do with their demonic nature. They only happen to receive this prohibition because they are as supernatural beings able to understand Jesus' divine nature. For the features noted as characteristic of the prohibition to the demons, namely knowledge (the demons' confession) and the relation of the prohibition to the person of Jesus himself, are found also in another passage to which we must now turn: Jesus' silencing his disciples after the confession at Caesarea Philippi at 8:30.

## III

The composition of Mark 8:27–33 is difficult and the history of tradition behind it not easy to determine.[53] We are concerned with it only insofar as it is significant for the analysis of the silence command. The first task is to dig out the redactional parts. These are v. 27a;[54] v. 30;[55] v. 31aα;[56] v. 32a.[57] That leaves three pieces of tradition: Peter's confession, the announcement of suffering, and the Satan saying. The first two are each independent pieces of tradition.[58] When and how they came together is difficult to say with precision, but Peter's confession seems to have required very early on some climactic continuation in a reply by Jesus which heightened it.[59] (This does not necessarily mean that Mark drew upon an already existing connection between Peter's confession and a prophecy of the passion.)[60]

What is the meaning of the messianic confession and silence command? Lohmeyer[61] proposed that the silence command applied to the following announcement of the passion of the Son of Man which developed the messianic confession. On this view Jesus neither accepted nor rejected the messianic confession but let it stand as he had previously allowed the opinions of the people to stand. It is true that Mark relatively seldom uses the Christ title in key passages but only takes it over on occasion from the tradition.[62] However, Lohmeyer overlooks the fact that *kai ērxato didaskein* ("and he began to teach") is a common Marcan introductory formula.[63] So

v. 31 begins a new section and the silence command belongs with what precedes it, i.e. to the confession. This corresponds also to the previously noted position of the silence commands after the description of what is to be kept silent. But the parallels at 1:34 and 3:11f clearly imply that a silence command is an indirect affirmation of what has preceded. What must be kept quiet is true rather than not yet fully valid.[64] So Mark here understood the Christ title as a valid definition of Jesus' nature. This corresponds also to 14:61.[65] We can only surmise why he here uses the title Christ rather than Son of God. It was probably there in the tradition, fitting well as an antithesis to the belief of the crowd in Jesus as Elijah, or John the Baptist, i.e. as a forerunner.

So 8:30 is a complete parallel to 1:34 and 3:11f and shows us that the silence command in those passages cannot be explained by reference to the special nature of the demons.[66] It is, however, of course very significant that in 8:30 and from there on the disciples are initiated into the secret. The special knowledge that from now on the disciples have over other people consists in their hearing that the Son of God–Messiah must suffer as Son of Man.[67] This knowledge now distinguishes them from other people even though they do not yet understand it. It is this proclamation of the suffering of the Son of Man which Mark designates as "public" in contrast to "puzzling" talk. So the secret remains a secret. But after Caesarea Philippi it is one secret for the disciples and another for the rest. The people grope in the dark over the nature of Jesus; to them the Kingdom of God is a puzzle and they are amazed. The disciples by contrast know about Jesus' messiahship, and must now try to understand what it means that the Messiah must be a suffering Messiah.

It is plain, too, from other observations that after 8:27 the position of the disciples has changed.[68]

1 The next main section, 8:27—10:52, contains more explicit teaching to the disciples.[69] This includes especially all the passion predictions (8:27; 9:30f; 10:32b), the transfiguration (9:2, 9ff), the comment on the healing of the epileptic (9:28f), the discussions on rank (9:33; 10:35: cf. v. 41), the comment on the meeting with the young man (10:23f).

2 The reaction of the disciples to the deeds and words of Jesus becomes different. Whereas previously the reactions of both the disciples and the crowd are described by expressions of astonishment or fear,[70] this changes after 8:27. The same words continue to

predominate for the crowd,[71] but the disciples are distinguished from the crowd: they (the crowd) were astonished, whereas those who followed were afraid (10:32). Fear is the response of the disciples to the passion predictions (9:6, 32).[72] Whereas the crowd's attitude hardens into unbelieving astonishment – for Mark astonishment is an expression of unbelief which admittedly perceives the event of the miracle but does not understand, because it is hardened[73] – the disciples begin to fear, although they have not yet been granted any real understanding.

3 The observations which E. Schweizer collected on the significance of the "discipleship" motif in the major section 8:27—10:52 are also relevant.[74] To expand them slightly, the verb *akolouthein* ("to follow") is hardly ever in this section used in the simple sense of "go after someone" but always in the pregnant sense of "be a disciple of" (8:34; 9:38(?); 10:21, 28, 32, 52), whereas previously this was never the case (3:7; 5:24; 6:1(?), cf. 11:9; 14:13, 54) – except for the actual "sayings about discipleship". Correspondingly, Jesus appears as the "one who goes on ahead" (10:32; cf. 16:7). Mark seems to have chosen the material available to him with a quite definite viewpoint, namely the theme "discipleship".[75] Further, corresponding to the discipleship motif there is the motif *en tę̄ hodǭ* ("in the way") which emerges throughout the section in redactional contexts (8:27; 9:33f;[76] 10:32, 52). In view of this, the remaining occurrences of *hodos* ("way") in this section can be said to gain a similar resonance (10:17, 46; cf.11:8), since *hodos* is at the same time both the way up to Jerusalem (10:32), and the way of suffering (8:27; 9:33; 10:32, always in connection with the passion predictions). There is also a question whether Mark understood the citation which introduces his Gospel (1:2f) in terms of the way of suffering. The placing of the destiny of the Baptist in parallel with that of Jesus would count in favour of the suggestion.[77] In all other passages in the Gospel the word *hodos* comes from the tradition and is not used with reference to the way of Jesus. Further, in the section 8:27— 10:52 there are no miracle stories although these have dominated the first main section. 9:14–29 and 10:46–52 are only apparently counter-evidence. Mark has reshaped 9:14–29 on the basis of a motif already there (9:18b) into an instruction of the disciples about the relationship between the authority of Jesus and that of the disciples (9:28f redactional). And the healing of blind Bartimaeus is made into a discipleship story by its redactional framework (vv. 46, 52d).

4 Finally we must touch on the motif of the disciples' lack of under-

standing which Wrede himself brought into his study on the messianic secret.[78] It is found throughout the entire first and second parts of the Gospel,[79] but apparently with characteristic differences. 4:13b (I take the second part of the verse to be redactional)[80] relates the disciples' lack of understanding to "all parables"; 6:52[81] relates it to the feeding miracles; 7:18 to the saying of Jesus in v. 15; 8:17ff again to the feeding miracle. On the other hand, the second part focuses the disciples' lack of understanding christologically.[82] Twice it is related to the suffering of the Son of Man: in 8:32b taking up a fragment of tradition, and also at 9:32. If we include 9:10 here too that gives us another case of concentration on Christology, this time on the resurrection. There is no need to interpret 9:6 here; it is simply a redactional note on v. 5, a verse which does not fit Mark's conception.[83]

So what does the messianic secret consist of for Mark? We can now formulate it more exactly. It is indeed Jesus' messiahship, or as Mark would say in his own terms, Jesus' divine sonship, which remains hidden from the world and is known only to the demons – due to their supernatural knowledge – and since Caesarea Philippi to the disciples – through the miracle of Jesus' authority which they repeatedly experienced. But the disciples can only experience Jesus' messiahship in connection with his suffering. Mark therefore attaches the first passion prediction to Peter's confession and works both up into a single pericope. This suffering remains incomprehensible to the disciples until the cross. Only there, in the light of Jesus' death, is full understanding and genuine confession of Jesus' divine sonship possible, as Mark shows by way of example through the gentile centurion's confession at the cross.[84]

If we try now to verify this interpretation by reference to the one remaining passage, Mark 9:9, it does not seem at once all to come undone. At first sight it seems very different from Mark 8:30, even though both passages are redactional creations of the evangelist.[85] In 8:30 the silence command concerns the messiahship of Jesus, as Peter has formulated it in his confession. 9:9 gives the content of what is to be kept silent in quite general terms with *ha eidon* ("what they had seen"). In 8:31ff the messiahship is described by the passion prediction. In 9:9 by contrast the resurrection is singled out and a temporal limit set to the messianic secret.

However, the differences are really not so significant as might at first sight appear. Even though the difficult problems about the history of the tradition in 9:2–8 are far from solved it seems to me probable that by his additions Mark revised a hellenistic version of an originally Palestinian legend.[86] It seems to me certain that for Mark the point of this worked-over legend lay in the heavenly proclamation of Jesus' divine sonship, i.e. in v. 7, and not for example in the appearance of Moses and Elijah. This seems clear on various grounds. Mark interprets divine sonship as a metamorphosis of a human figure; he weakens v. 5 by his redactional v. 6; finally there is the parallel with Mark 1:9–11, the baptism narrative, which occupies roughly the same position in the first part of the Gospel as this does in the second. *ha eidon* ("what they had seen") therefore probably refers to the proclamation of Jesus' divine sonship itself, to which everything which the disciples "saw" points. On the other hand, crucifixion and resurrection belong so closely together for Mark that in his understanding the resurrection is virtually included in the crucifixion. Unfortunately this hypothesis cannot here be supported in the necessary detail; it would need an interpretation of Mark's crucifixion narrative. We can only mention a few points out of our section: it is no coincidence that Mark interprets the tradition's prophecies of the passion and resurrection only as passion prophecies. For that is all the repudiation of Peter at 8:32f and the first discipleship saying at 8:34 can refer to. And only then is the saying about greatest and least (9:33–5), and the corresponding passage, 10:35–45, explicable in terms of the kerygma. It is also notable that at 9:12b Mark takes up the Son of Man announcement again with a passion prophecy and also understands Elijah as a suffering figure (v. 12a, 13).[87] Finally, the confession of the centurion at the cross (15:39)[88] can only be connected with 9:9 if Mark saw crucifixion and resurrection as a basic unity.

So Mark 9:9 does not contradict Mark 8:30, but interprets it.[89] That the silence command is lifted and abolished only by the resurrection means that Jesus' majesty can only be understood in the light of the cross which is united with the resurrection. That this is so is shown by the way Mark's Gospel continues, especially in the passion narrative, where the disciples are shown as lacking understanding and without courage.[90] Then the divine answer to the cross finally grants understanding to a bystander.

## IV

To conclude: a look at what is usually called the "messianic secret" in Mark has shown that there are really two phenomena: the messianic secret, under the constraint of which the demons and after

Caesarea Philippi the disciples stand; and the miracle secret which cannot be kept and shows that Jesus' miracles press onward into the public realm of proclamation. Both motifs have starting-points in the tradition, but in their present form they are both redactional. Both have at first a quite different meaning, even though they are not wholly unrelated. For the messianic secret also is broken during Jesus' lifetime (cf. 10:46ff; 11:1ff; 12:1ff, especially v. 12b), and the miracle secret also may echo the motif that Jesus' miracles can be understood only from the perspective of the cross and resurrection. Admittedly this cannot be demonstrated, but the similar formulation of both types of command,[91] suggests that they should not be too sharply differentiated. There is, however, a fundamental theological difference, because regardless of all kinds of converging motifs, the secrecy motif embraces different contents and indicates theologically two different things: the miracle secret points to the power of Jesus' miracles which cannot remain hidden because it is the sign of the messianic age; the messianic secret qualifies the nature of Jesus' messiahship which must be understood kerygmatically, i.e. from the perspective of the cross and resurrection, if it is to be really understood. Or to put it in another way, the messianic secret warns against interpreting the historical Jesus independently of the cross and resurrection because any such understanding of Jesus' authority can only have the character of a satanic temptation. The miracle secret on the other hand leads back to the historical Jesus, because his authority and action simply press upon the onlooker, whether he wants this or not – and even if he does not understand it. Or to put it in yet another way: Jesus' authority and deed admittedly lead only to unbelieving astonishment; but in Mark's conception this astonishment is for the confessing believer a pointer to Jesus' messiahship.

So Mark seems to harness two christological ideas. One could be seen as tending in the direction of the hellenistic *theios anēr* ("divine man") conception, the other as attempting to make theological sense of the messianic material from the perspective of the cross. The difficulty is that both, although present in differing degrees in the tradition, are Marcan. They cannot be put aside as mere tradition. This raises again the question of their theological unity and the relationship between these two ideas. That can be made more exact by asking whether Mark provides any help towards interpreting their dialectical relationship more precisely.

The kerygmatic summary of Jesus' preaching at 1:15, by which Mark with the help of traditional formulations [92] prefaces his Gospel, seems to have a related structure. It is put together out of the indications of the new time, the time grasped by the Kingdom of God – "The time is fulfilled and the kingdom of God has drawn near!" – and the challenge to seize this time: "Repent and believe in the gospel." "Gospel", an expression which characteristically occurs mainly in the second half of Mark, designates the presence of Jesus with his community.[93] Mark knows very well that this presence always leads to suffering.[94] The first part of this kerygmatic statement of the preaching proclaims the new age when the Kingdom of God is near; the second part calls for a correct attitude to this new time, for faith in the gospel. The first (1:16—8:26) and the second (8:27—10:52 [13:37]) parts of Mark's Gospel stand in a similar relationship. The first part describes the new time breaking into the world, with the main emphasis on the miracles and the parables of the Kingdom. The second part bears witness that the new time can only be grasped and understood in discipleship leading to suffering.

This structural combination of miracle secret and messianic secret is thus not without analogy elsewhere in Mark's Gospel. The combination of glory which cannot remain hidden, but which is for that very reason not understood, and suffering through following in the way of the cross, which alone can reveal the majesty of Jesus – this combination of miracle secret which cannot remain secret because it really is miracle, and messianic secret which must remain a mystery to the world – this combination is necessary, and finds in Mark's passion its most condensed form. There the majesty of Jesus is first made recognizable (14:61f, 15:39) through its deepest concealment, through his trial and cross. The Marcan Christology is thus to be understood as an attempt not to remove the *theios anēr* ("divine man") Christology and the manifestation idea of the hellenistic community, but to make it comprehensible from the perspective of the kerygma of the cross. There it is precisely the combination of the miracle whose reality cannot remain hidden, and the uncomprehending astonishment of an unbelieving world in the face of this miracle, which becomes a witness for faith.

## NOTES

1 Cf. n.1 of the previous essay (by E. Schweizer).

2 Conzelmann, 1968, 43.

3 The eschatological material is almost exclusively limited to the synoptic apocalypse of Mark 13 which Mark found available to him in essentially its present form. In addition cf. 8:38f (on this see Schweizer, above, p. 72, n.29);

12:9; 14:62. The synoptic apocalypse in Mark is quite isolated and Mark never gives advance references to it in the course of his Gospel as he does for the passion. These are the main reasons, along with the minimal redactional activity in Mark 13 and the "eschatological" interpretation of the cross at 15:33ff, why I am sceptical about the thesis of E. Trocmé, 1975, 215ff, who sees in Mark 13 the climax and end of the original Gospel.

4 This can perhaps be assumed from individual pericopae, such as the last supper reports, and the crucifixion narrative in Mark 15:20ff. On this cf. U. Wilckens, "Hellenistisch-christliche Missionsüberlieferung und Jesustradition", *TLZ* 89 (1964) 519. Also E. Trocmé, 1975, 61ff.

5 Do the numerous, mostly redactional – cf. above, pp. 78ff – notes after the miracle stories, that they spread abroad the news about Jesus, contain a pointer back to the original *Sitz im Leben* of the miracle stories, namely proclamation itself?

6 Cf. Mark 8:34ff; 10:39; 13:11ff; 15:16ff, 21.

7 I would thus see the origin of Mark rather differently from E. Schweizer 1964a, 1964b; cf. also Schweizer "Die Frage nach dem historischen Jesus", *EvT* 24 (1964) 403–8. The alternatives which Mark has to choose between are not a hellenistic kerygma theology whose kerygma has largely cut loose from Jesus Christ and become a kerygmatic counter, and a Jewish–Christian theology which, like Q, understands Jesus as *the* teacher. There probably were, as the structure of the pre-Pauline communities clearly shows (on this, W. Schmithals, "Paulus und der historische Jesus", *ZNW* 53 (1962) 156f), some hellenistic communities which knew only a little about the historical Jesus. But Mark comes from a different (Galilean?) hellenistic community which has and uses traditions about Jesus Christ. This community is described by D. Georgi, *Die Gegner des Paulus im 2 Korintherbrief* (1964) 210ff, especially 213f, in my opinion on the whole convincingly, even if the evangelist Mark must be distinguished from it. The materials taken up by Mark into his Gospel have in my opinion almost all been revised in a hellenistic milieu. They do not come to the evangelist direct from Jewish Christian tradition. So the theological achievement of Mark consists not in the fact of taking up pre-Easter Jesus tradition, nor in the selection of this material (Mark probably used everything he knew, as his use of chapter 13 and also 11:27ff shows), but in the manner of his total composition. That means that if the messianic secret should turn out to be a significant piece of Marcan theology it must at the same time also be significant for the total conception of the Gospel. In putting the question this way E. Bickermann (1923) is right.

8 On the method of vocabulary statistics cf. J. Schreiber, "Der Kreuzigungsbericht des Markusevangeliums" (Bonn Dissertation, 1958, 97ff). Also E. Schweizer, 1963, 93ff. Naturally this kind of investigation makes sense only within certain limits. For example, it is likely that Mark received some traditions only orally and then formulated them using his "own" words. But in combination with other methods it gives criteria for ascertaining more precisely the nature of the pre-Marcan tradition.

9 *Akolouthein* ("to follow") is frequent in Mark (19 occurrences; 25 in Matt.; 17 in Luke). Of these passages 3:7; 6:1; 10:52 and probably also 2:15; 10:32 are redactional. *ochlos polys* ("a great crowd") is redactional at 5:21; 6:34; 8:1; 9:14;

12:37. Cf. also 2:13; 3:9, 20; 4:1; 7:14, 17; 8:34; 10:1; 11:18; 12:12. v. 24b is more difficult to judge: *synthlibein* ("to throng") occurs again in the tradition at v. 31, but cf. also 3:9. But other linguistic peculiarities of Mark also make it improbable that the passage 5:25–34 was available to Mark in written form: *euthus* ("immediately"); *mastix* ("plague", cf. 3:10); *haptomai* ("I touch") (cf. 3:10; 6:56); *sōzomai* ("I save", cf. 6:56 and Lohmeyer's *Commentary*, 104). On all this cf. similarly A. Meyer, *Die Entstehung des Markusevangeliums*, Festgabe for A. Jülicher, 1927, 40.

10 See below, p. 84.

11 *Prosormizomai* ("I moor"), Gennesaret, *peritrechein* ("to run around"), *asthenein* ("to be sick") do not occur elsewhere in Mark and some of them do not occur elsewhere in the whole NT. *agros* ("country") *krabbatos* ("bed") occur only in Mark's tradition. Otherwise the vocabulary statistics support the view that it is redactional.

12 The typically redactional phrases, "all those who were sick", "all the city", are worth noting.

13 Cf. R. Bultmann, 1963, 224 and especially 422 in the supplement. Also M. Dibelius, 1934, 94. And E. Sjöberg, 1955, 112 n.1.

14 7.33aα could be redactional. *Ochlos* ("crowd") (cf. n.9 above) and *kat' idiān* ("privately"; see 4:34; 6:31f; 9:2, 8; 13:3) support this suggestion.

15 Cf. Bultmann, 1963, 221.

16 After conservative research had always searched behind the messianic secret for as much tradition as possible to go back to Jesus (cf. for example V. Taylor, 1948, 148ff, and 1952 throughout), it is above all the merit of E. Sjöberg, 1955, to have drawn attention to the question of the tradition standing behind Mark's redactional understanding of the messianic secret. Admittedly he defined the messianic secret concept far too widely and this prevented his investigation of the pre-Marcan tradition from achieving any precision.

17 By the demon remaining completely passive and only the mother, the Syro-Phoenician woman, emerging in an active role, all the typical traits of an exorcism disappear.

18 Verse 43a is certainly redactional (cf. nn. 24, 28, 31), whereas v. 43b contains the original "demonstration" of the miracle. So we have a silence command without any reference to the subsequent spreading of the news of the miracle. This is the only visible exception in Mark's treatment of the miracle stories. How should it be understood? We may point out that a breaking of the silence command here would have made the heavily redacted rejection at Nazareth scene which follows almost impossible. It seems to me most probable that a raising from the dead was so strong a testimony to Jesus' messiahship that a veiling was necessary here if the dialectic between revelation and hiddenness described on p. 87 was to be preserved.

19 Cf. the readings provided by D q Θ ϕ C K, which apart from their differences from one another also betray their dependence on the text represented by B (Vaticanus) by the *eis tēn kōmēn* ("into the village") which is generally retained.

20 Cf. Schniewind, *Commentary*, 1963, 145; Grundmann, *Commentary*, 1973, 220f; Schweizer, 1964a, 351 [cf. 1964b, 428].

21 Cf. also A. Kuby, 1958, 58; T. A. Burkill, 1963, 149f.

22 On Mark 5:43 see above n. 18.

23 *Kērussein* ("to preach") is in my opinion redactional in all 12 Marcan instances, the only debatable cases being 1:4, 7; *erēmos topos* ("desert place") occurs apart from 4 redactional passages only at 6:35 in the tradition (formulated by Mark?). Elsewhere the tradition speaks only of *erēmos* ("desert"). Mark uses this noun alone only once, following up an OT quotation (1:4).

24 Adverbial *polla* ("many things") 4:2; 6:34; cf. 3:12; 5:43. Also probably a further 6 times in the tradition. *exerchesthai* ("to come out") 1:28, 29, 35, 38; 2:13; 3:6; 6:1, 12, 34(?), 54; 7:31; 8:11, 27; 9:30; 11:11f(?); the remaining 23 instances are more likely to belong to the tradition, many of them referring to demons. *archesthai* ("to begin"): 4:1; 5:20; 6:2, 34(?), 55; 8:31; 10:28(?), 32, 41(?); 12:1; in the remaining 16 passages more likely tradition. *ho logos* ("the word") used absolutely: 2:2; 4:33; 8:32. It stems from tradition in the interpretation of the parable of the sower. *hōste* ("so that") with infinitive: 3:10, 20; 4:1. Also 7 times in passages coming from the tradition. *dynasthai* ("to be able"): 3:20; 4:33; 7:24; 9:28; 10:26(?), and 27 times probably from the tradition. On *eiserchesthai* ("to enter"), see above, p. 78; *pros auton* ("to him") i.e. Jesus: 1:32; 2:13; 3:8, 13; 4:1; 7:1; 10:1; 11:27; 12:18, and also 8 times from the tradition.

25 *Embrimasthai* ("to be angry"), twice, and *horān* ("to see"), three times, are rare in Mark and always come from the tradition. *kai legei* ("and he says") is redactional at 1:38 and otherwise probably from the tradition.

26 Redactional, referring to exorcisms: 1:34, 39; 3:15; 9:28.

27 Double negative with *mē* ("not") otherwise only at 11:14.

28 5:43; 7:36; 8:26, 30; 9:9. Four of these are in the dative.

29 Egerton papyrus 2f. I[r] (in Hennecke–Wilson, *New Testament Apocrypha* i, 96f). According to Jeremias (p. 95 in that volume) the author knew all the canonical Gospels but reproduced them from memory so that oral tradition may well also have had some influence.

30 See above, n. 24.

31 On *kērussein* ("to proclaim") see above, n. 23; on *mēdeni* ("to no one") n. 28; *diastellesthai* ("to charge") 5:43; 9:9; 8:15 is questionable; *hosos* ("how great, many") 3:8, 10; 5:20; 6:30, 56; 9:13. The other seven occurrences are tradition.

32 Cf. Dibelius, 1934, 57f.

33 *Hyperperissōs* ("beyond measure") occurs only here in the NT. The perfect tense of *poiein* ("to do") is tradition; Mark prefers the aorist – see below, n. 43. *poiein* ("to do") with accusative and infinitive is found elsewhere only at 1:17. *kōphos* ("deaf") and *alalos* ("dumb") are found elsewhere only in the healing of the epileptic boy, at 9:17, 25. Cf. Isa. 35:5; Wis. 10:21.

34 On the place names see below, n. 54.

35 Against Bickermann, 1923, 132f, who wants to divide Mark's miracles into "easy" (public) and impossible (secret) ones. At best the interpretation of 5:21–4, 35–43 might contain a starting-point for this idea.

36 This tells against the thesis of Bousset, 1970, 107, and Dibelius 1934, 223f, that the messianic secret provides an explanation for Jesus' lack of success.

37 It is perhaps clear that this interpretation of the miracle secret is quite close to the interpretation of the messianic secret by H. J. Ebeling, 1939. As a matter of fact I believe that Ebeling was in many respects correct, especially in trying to understand the miracle stories which carried a silence command, in the light of the miracle stories as such. But he did not see the difference in content between the miracle secret and the actual messianic secret idea, and so generalized his thesis in a way which did violence to the evidence.

38 There is also redactional activity as early as v. 27. At any rate up to v. 27a the narrative contains all the motifs required for an exorcism. The vocabulary of v. 28 is redactional. On *exerchesthai* ("to come out") see above, n. 24. On *euthus* ("immediately") see Schmidt, 1919, 50f. *akoē* ("report") and *pantachou* ("everywhere") admittedly occur nowhere else in Mark's redaction, but *holos ho* ("all the") is a typical redactional phrase. Cf. Schweizer 1963, 97, and 1:33, 39 (!); 6:55; 14:9, which all tell the extent of the proclamation. Galilee is perhaps added redactionally at 1:16 too (Lohmeyer, 1963, 31; Grundmann, 1973, 39). Cf. 1:14, 39; 3:7; 7:31; 9:30; 14:28 (?); 15:41; 16:7. It is undoubtedly a word which expresses a Marcan motif.

39 Cf. Lohmeyer, 1963, 99; on the various attempts to demarcate the redactional material, cf. Bultmann, 1963, 419 (supplement to 210). Burkill, 1963, 94f considers vv. 18–20 to be tradition. Wrede, 1971, 140f, interprets it in terms of the secret.

40 Apart from the words already discussed – *kērussein* ("to proclaim") n. 23; *archesthai* ("to begin") n. 24; *hosos* ("how great, many") n. 31; – Decapolis is also probably redactional at 7:31. *thaumazein* ("to wonder") is certainly redactional again at 6:6 and probably also at 15:44. But the decisive argument for the redactional character of v. 20 concerns the corrections (see below, nn. 41–3) which make it virtually impossible to follow R. H. Lightfoot, 1935, 88ff, Dibelius, 1934, 74, Taylor, 1952, *ad loc.* in taking all three verses as Marcan.

41 *Kērussein* ("to proclaim") instead of apangellein ("to announce").

42 Jesus instead of God.

43 *Poiein* ("to do") never occurs in the perfect tense in the redaction, but does in the tradition. Cf. 5:33; 7:37; 11:17, etc. The aorist is very frequently redactional, cf. only e.g. 3:14, 16; 6:30; 9:13; 14:9. It is rare in the tradition: 2:25; 14:8. In the passage under consideration Mark has changed the tradition's perfect tense into an aorist.

44 For a hellenistic example, compare the story of Chonsu, the God who drives out demons, in R. Reitzenstein, *Hellenistische Wundererzählungen*, 1963², 124. For a Jewish example, the story of Rabbi Schimeon ben Jochai in Billerbeck, *Kommentar zum NT aus Talmud und Midrasch*, 1922–, vol. iv, 535, or the story of Rabbi Hanina ben Dosa and the female demon Agrath in P. Fiebig, *Rabbinische Wundergeschichten*, 1933, 7.

45 Cf. the evidence assembled by R. Reitzenstein, *Poimandres*, 1904, 20f, especially the magical prayer of Astrampsychos. On this see O. Bauernfeind, *Die Worte der Dämonen im Markusevangelium*, 1927, 14.

46 Evidence in Blass-Debrunner-Funk, *A Greek Grammar of the NT* (Chicago, 1961), § 346; Klostermann, *Commentary*, 1950, on Mark 1:25, *Papyri Osloenses* I, ed. S. Eitrem, 1925, 76f at 164. Mark perhaps understood *phīmousthai* ("to be muzzled") in terms of the messianic secret, in contrast to its meaning in the earlier tradition.

47 Cf. Mark 4:39.

48 On the significance of *phīmoun* ("to muzzle"), cf. Burkill, 1963, 72.

49 The demons' self-mutilation means that they have recognized Jesus; since it is *alalon* ("dumb") (v. 17), it cannot of course make confession.

50 Cf. Bultmann, 1963, 223.

51 Cf. on this E. Schweizer, article *"Huios theou"* ("Son of God") in *TDNT*, vol. viii, on Mark 5.7.

52 The secrecy theory would then be the hermeneutical presupposition of Mark's Christology, not of the gospel genre (cf. Conzelmann, above n. 2). Matthew and Luke also belong to the gospel genre.

53 On this see now F. Hahn, *The Titles of Jesus in Christology* (1963, ET London: Lutterworth, 1969) 223–8; E. Haenchen, "Die Komposition von Mk 8.27–9.1 und Par", *Nov T* 6 (1963) 81–109; E. Dinkler, "Peter's Confession and the 'Satan' Saying: The Problem of Jesus' Messiahship", in *The Future of our Religious Past*, ed. J. M. Robinson, 1971, 169–202.

54 On *exerchesthai* ("to come out") cf. n. 24. On *en tę̄ hodǭ* ("in the way"), below, p. 84. *Mathētai* ("disciples") does not necessarily tell against the verse being redaction, although Mark frequently uses *hoi dōdeka* ("the twelve") for the disciples. The word is found in both tradition and redaction. On *kōmē* ("village") cf. above, p. 78. Where the place-name Caesarea Philippi comes from is hard to say. But it certainly cannot be used as an argument for the historicity of the scene. On that basis many passages with even less common place-names could be judged historical, for example the marriage at Cana! It is worth pondering that in the preceding section Mark occasionally introduces unusual place-names in redactional sections (7:24, 31; 8:10, 22). It is doubtful whether a "journey" into Gentile territory can be reconstructed. In 7:24–30 the scene is laid by the tradition too (v. 26!). Nevertheless the trip to Phoenicia is surely meant to be programmatic in view of the significance for Mark of the proclamation to the Gentiles (one has only to consider 13:10 and 15:39). In itself Caesarea Philippi is a quite well known area which Mark might have chosen because he wanted to have Peter's confession taken place on the border of Gentile territory (cf. A. Schlatter, *Der Evangelist Matthäus*, 1929, 502).

55 Cf. 3:12; 7:36.

56 On *archesthai* ("to begin"), n. 24. On *didaskein* ("to teach"), Schweizer, 1963, 95f, cf. esp. 4:1; 6:2, 34.

57 Cf. especially 2:2; 4:33, further for *lalein* ("to speak") 1:34; 4:34; 12:1; 14:9, 43 (?). On *parrēsia* ("openly") cf. Schweizer, above, p. 69. Hahn (n. 53), 224 considers 32b redactional too. But in my opinion that cannot be demonstrated.

58 Against Bultmann, 1963, 258, cf. Hahn (n. 53) 223.

59 John 6:66–71 and *Gos. Thomas* 13 each show one answer by Jesus. The same is true of Matt. 16:13ff, since Matthew's special material in vv. 17ff must surely have been preceded by some such scene as Peter's confession, which is perhaps still echoed in the full title "Son of the living God" in v. 16. It is, however, important that this answer is in each case different. If Mark found in the tradition available to him an answer by Jesus also, and that remains possible, he has replaced it with the silence command. Cf. Dinkler (n. 53) 184ff.

60 Against Schweizer, 1963, 68, there seem to me to be in 8:27–33 at least two pericopae which did not originally belong together. The following reasons seem to me to argue for this: (1) If the redactional link phrases between the pieces of tradition are cut out there is at any rate between 8:29 and 31a*β* no further connection. And only if v. 32b is original (cf. n. 57) is there any between v. 31 and v. 33. It is not very likely that Mark would have replaced an existing connection between v. 29 and v. 31a*β* with his own redactional introduction 31a*α*, since Mark prefers to use the word *didaskein* ("to teach") at the start of a new piece of tradition: 1:21f; 2:13; 4:1f; 6:2, 6, 34; 9:31; 10:1; 12:35. (2) It seems to me more probable that the three pieces of tradition do not have the same origin. Verses 27b–29 (cf. Mark 6:14ff) come from the Palestinian Aramaic-speaking area. This is supported by the expectations of a forerunner, the phrase *eipan ... legontes* ("they said ... saying") which is so difficult that in my opinion it can only be explained in terms of the Aramaic (elsewhere only at 12:26), the semitic predication *su ei* ("you are") (E. Norden, *Agnostos Theos*, 1956[4], 177ff). H. E. Tödt, *The Son of Man in the Synoptic Tradition* (ET London: SCM; Philadelphia: Westminster, 1965), especially 201f, has considered the origin of the passion prophecies. The connection of the Messiah with the future Son of Man in Mark 14:61f seems to be earlier in the history of the tradition than this connection with the suffering one (E. Dinkler, 1971, 185). The Satan word to Peter seems to me as to Bultmann, 1963, 258, n. 2, to be a hellenistic construction, since the linguistic counter-arguments adduced in M. Black, *An Aramaic Approach to the Gospels and Acts* (1954[2]) 263f do not stand up: *hypage* ("go!") is vulgar Greek, cf. Liddell-Scott, *Lexicon*, BII; *Satanas* ("Satan") can be adequately explained from a familiarity with the LXX; *phronein ta tou theou*, etc. ("to mind the things of God") is in my opinion scarcely conceivable in Aramaic; *phronein* with accusative plural neuter is typical vulgar Greek, whereas the Aramaic *dî* ("that") for *ta tou* ("the things of") as in the Peshitta, is uncommon, as the parallels adduced in Billerbeck i 748 show, against Dinkler, 1971, 186: polemic against Peter was at least possible in hellenistic Christian circles, as is shown by Gal. 2; Mark 14:66f; John 20:1ff. Cf. Bultmann (as above) and J. Schreiber, 1961, 177, esp. n. 1; rather differently, G. Klein, "Die Verleugnung des Petrus", *ZTK* 58 (1961) 325. These considerations also place question-marks against the reconstruction of Dinkler, 1971, 185ff, where v. 33b is attached to the messianic confession. Dinkler's analysis has not yet fully convinced me here, attractive though it is, and in my opinion preferable, on account of its greater simplicity and compactness, to the reconstruction of Hahn (n. 53) 224f.

Be that as it may, if Mark was the first to combine at least 27b–29 and 31 – and this is supported also by the parallels in Mark's special material, John and Gos. Thomas, which clearly knew nothing of a link like Matthew's – then the sequence "messianic secret – passion prophecy" gains very great theological weight, because the statement that Jesus' messiahship can only be understood together with the suffering of the Son of Man becomes Mark's most characteristic theological achievement.

61 *Commentary*, 1963, 165.

62 Redactional only at 1:1 (?) and 14:61 (?).

63 See above, n. 60.

64 So too Haenchen (n. 53), 87.

65 Against O. Cullmann, *The Christology of the New Testament*, 1959, 122ff.

66 This counts against the thesis of Bauernfeind (n. 45 above).

67 The significance of the title "Son of Man" for the evangelist Mark can only be determined with difficulty, since Mark has only used it in traditional contexts. Did he still understand it at all? For the Son of Man title seems not to come under the messianic secret (2:10, 28). The suffering Son of Man occurs simply in the context of instruction to the disciples. Mark probably thought of a side of the Son of Man comprehensible only to the disciples.

68 Against Wrede, 1971, 115ff, Sjöberg, 1955, 103, emphasizes the central position of Caesarea Philippi.

69 Cf. Lohmeyer, 1963, 161.

70 Referring to the crowd: 5:20 *thaumazein* ("to marvel"); 7:37 *ekplēssesthai* ("to be astonished"); (referring to the disciples: 6:51 *existasthai* ("to be amazed") is tradition, but is interpreted by Mark; cf. in addition the passages from the tradition: 1:27 (*thambeisthai*, "to be amazed"); 2:15; 5:42 (*existasthai*); 4:41; 5:15 (*phobeisthai*, "to fear").

71 9:15 *ekthambeisthai*, "to be greatly amazed"; 10:32 *thambeisthai*. Cf. 11:18; 12:17.

72 *thambeisthai* is used of the disciples only at 10:24, but there relates to a special proclamation of Jesus.

73 In a redactional note at 6:52 Mark explains what he means by *existasthai*.

74 Schweizer, 1964a, 349ff [cf. 1964b, 427ff].

75 I can scarcely believe that Mark 8:27—10:52 simply puts together unsorted material. Rather, every pericope is related to the theme of "discipleship". But on this cf. Schweizer, 1964a, 351.

76 K. L. Schmidt, 1919, 230, rightly observes that v. 35 constitutes a second more original beginning to the following pericope. But the history of the tradition is not clear. Verse 34b seems to depend on something which should really have been related before. The vocabulary provides no clear guidance. The parallel in 8:16 suggests a redactor at work, but the poor construction of these two verses is not explained by the supposition of a purely redactional formation.

77 Consider *paradothēnai* ("to be delivered up") at 1:14; *metanoia* ("repentance") at 1:4, 15; *kērussein* ("to proclaim") at 1:4, 14.

78 Wrede, 1971, 92ff.

79 On its special frequency in chaps. 6–8 cf. Schweizer, 1963, 100 n. 32.

80 Cf. Schweizer, above, p. 68.

81 Cf. above n. 73. Cf. further on *sunienai* ("to understand") 7:14; 8:17(!), 21.

82 Cf. on this Kuby, 1958, 54.

83 Mark 9:5, 18f; 10:35ff, 41ff are from the tradition and should not be used automatically to show Mark's understanding of the disciples. Cf. Sjöberg, 1955, 106.

85 I should note here that the women's reaction at Mark 16:8 remains a puzzle to me. Not even the origin of the half-verse (is 8c redaction?) is clear. There is at any rate a contradiction with 9:9. To assume that Mark is polemicizing

against a theology which ascribes to the resurrection – cut loose from the cross – power to proclaim with understanding, is difficult after 9:9, despite 15:39. It is unlikely that he intends playing off the gentile centurion against the women, since he inserted them redactionally at 15:40f, 47 and characterizes them positively (*ēkolouthoun*, "they used to follow"; *diēkonoun*, "they used to serve"; though *apo makrothen*, "from afar". Cf. on that 14:54!). It remains possible that Mark is using the women's fear, without direct polemic, to point back to the main thing, namely away from the story of the tomb and to the cross, 15:33–9. Or would a once existing old ending to Mark containing further appearances have clarified the passage? We do not know.

85 On the vocabulary, cf. above, n. 28 (on *mēdeis*, "no one") and n. 31 (on *diastellesthai*, "to charge"). 9b seems to point back to 8:31, though the addition of *ek nekrōn* ("from dead") admittedly remains unclear.

86 For analysis cf. Hahn, 1969, 334ff.

87 A hint from E. Schweizer. For the congruence of our view at this point, cf. Schweizer, above, p. 72, n. 29.

88 On the redactional character of this passage, see J. Schreiber (n. 8), 76, 114f.

89 Thus 9:9 does not have the central place that Wrede, 1971, 76f, and Conzelmann, 1968, 43, thought. Similarly Sjöberg, 1955, 105f.

90 Cf. Gethsemane, Peter's denial (which was perhaps placed here by Mark to accentuate the contrast between Jesus and his disciples; cf. P. Winter, *On the Trial of Jesus* (1961) 23f), and the total absence of the disciples in chap. 15 (cf. v. 40f).

91 And 5:43!

92 *Metanoein* ("to repent") cf. 1:4, the nearness of the *basileia* ("kingdom") and the fulfilment of time are motifs in the tradition.

93 Cf. W. Marxsen, *The Evangelist Mark* (1969), 117.

94 8:35; 10:29; cf. 13:10 with 11ff.

7

# The Quest for Wrede's Secret Messiah*

WILLIAM C. ROBINSON JR

William Wrede wanted to understand the secrecy motifs in the Gospel of Mark, Jesus' commands to the demons to be silent after they had addressed him with christological titles, his orders to disciples and others not to tell of his miracles, indications that he sought privacy, that he taught in parables to disclose the mystery of the Kingdom of God to insiders and conceal it from others, and that even the disciples – despite repeated private instruction – failed to understand. What Wrede accomplished is of importance sufficient to insure his book its place as a classic in NT research, and yet the inadequacies of his argument are such that it does not deserve the influence it still exerts on current efforts to interpret the Gospel of Mark. Wrede was remarkably perceptive as to the principles which should govern historical research into earliest Christianity, but by abandoning his first principle he failed to understand how the data he studied function in the Gospel of Mark. That task therefore remains to be done.

He saw that the gospel writers had to be understood in the social matrix of the communities of faith in which they lived and wrote, that the materials they used had not only survived in the Christian common life but also had been moulded and modified by their *Sitz im Leben* of the Church. He recognized that the evangelists were other than just recorders; they were spokesmen for their faith, so that understanding of the Gospels requires attention to their intentions in writing. That meant the Gospels are primary sources for the evangelists' views but only secondary sources for what they tell of Jesus' life. Even these few items indicate Wrede was operating with the principles which later guided both form criticism and redac-

* A review of *The Messianic Secret* by William Wrede. First published in *Int* 27 (1973) 10–30.

tion criticism. Not only did these insights give his work a future, to that extent ensuring its stature as a classic, but Wrede applied them consistently enough to put an end to the then dominant phase of gospel research, the nineteenth century's quest of the historical Jesus (the *Leben-Jesu Bewegung*), so that the book marks the close of an epoch in the history of the discipline and provided stimuli (along with the work of Wellhausen and others) for new directions.

Put in emotive terms the main effect of his book was to shock its readers with its implicit denial of Jesus' messianic self-consciousness (the sensitive issue in gospel research at the time); in methodological terms, it undermined the foundations on which the liberal lives of Jesus had been constructed. Wrede accused his colleagues of failing their first task, the historical assessment of the sources (4). To specify this charge he asserted three points (5–7): (1) An obvious rule of all critical historiography – too little observed in this case – is that what we actually possess is only a later narrator's view of Jesus' life, a view which is not identical with the thing itself. (2) One too quickly abandons the gospel account, substituting for it – by excising the incredible and arranging the residue – something the gospel writer never thought of and presenting this surrogate as if it were the historical substance of the gospel narratives. "The first task must always be the thorough illumination of the accounts in the spirit of those accounts themselves, to ask what the narrator in his own time wanted to say to his readers, and this task must be *carried to its conclusion* and made the foundation of critical historiography." (3) Third is the problem of psychological interpretation. Not that the use of psychology is in itself inappropriate, but it can be properly employed to help explain the development from one fact to another only when the facts are established *as* facts. Jesus research suffers from psychologizing guesswork.

Wrede presumably thought he was avoiding those errors by seeking first to understand what Mark wanted to say to his own readers (5f), but what Wrede actually did was formally very like the error of the old questers: before completing his analysis of Mark's intention he jumped over the Marcan text and landed in his own reconstruction of earliest Christianity. This is apparent from an analysis of his argument that Mark could not himself have invented the secrecy motif, even though it is rather widespread in his Gospel. Wrede claimed this conclusion is evident from the Gospel itself. In the Gospel of Mark secrecy motifs are presented in various ways and among them there is considerable inconsistency. Such inconsistency, Wrede maintained, could not be the work of a single individual (145).

Wrede's assertion is unambiguous, but when one searches his book for those inconsistencies which rule out Mark as originator of the secrecy motif, the results are initially puzzling, for instead of pointing out inconsistencies which are inconceivable for Mark, Wrede justified them: "Whether the idea existed is one thing; whether Mark carried it out with utter consistency is another. What would be incompatible in actual history might exist side by side in thought" (70; cf. 55f). Furthermore he pressed the point that contradictions are a necessary consequence of introducing the messianic secret into a Gospel: "For if the Evangelist had carried out this view strictly, if his Jesus had really kept himself utterly concealed, Mark would hardly have considered his life worth the telling" (125f). Nor can Wrede have meant the apparent inconsistency that Jesus' wish to remain unknown clashes with the statements that people disregarded his wishes and spread his fame anyway (1:45; 7:36f; 7:24); Wrede took these statements to be from Mark himself, so this inconsistency *is* due to a single person, Mark (127). Then, in a discussion of Mark as an author, Wrede concluded that Mark "did not really think from one point of his account to another" (132), that he had "little ability to put himself into the historical situation he presents.... Otherwise the scenes he presents could not contain such strange and – realistically viewed – such inconceivable things" (133). There is more (e.g., 111f, 237f), but it is of the same sort: Wrede has not really tried to show that a single individual was incapable of such variety of presentation; rather, in the case of Mark, he has shown the reverse.

One's initial perplexity at Wrede's claim that analysis of the Gospel of Mark shows Mark could not have originated the secrecy concept is resolved, I think, when one reaches the third section of his book (209ff), where Wrede presented his reconstruction of the historical origins of the messianic secret, a presentation prefaced (210) with a reference to his earlier claim to have shown that Mark did not invent the concept himself.

Wrede marshalled indications of the view in early Christianity that Jesus became the Messiah at the resurrection,[1] which he claims is the oldest view of which we have any knowledge (218), which arose not as Jesus' own view but as that of the Christian congregation on the basis of the appearances of the risen Christ (220). This earliest view gradually shifted as Jesus' past life received from it a new importance and dignity (218). The growing significance of Jesus' earthly life was to some extent paralleled by a decline in belief in the nearness of the parousia. From these lines of development the view that Jesus had been the Messiah gained substance, giving rise to a new, specifically Christian, messianic concept (219). The gospel writers are not at the end of this development but they are near its culmination: they, in contrast to Paul, narrate the life of the Messiah (223f).

Although Wrede might seem to have hedged somewhat in saying that when the secrecy concept arose, the original view of Jesus' life (by which Wrede meant a non-messianic view) was beginning to change, that hints of Jesus' future status were appearing in the stories of his life,[2] it was nonetheless his opinion that the secrecy concept arose when the traditions of Jesus were essentially non-christological.[3] Wrede's actual line of thought was, I think, as follows: hypothesis – the messianic secret arose at a point in the history of dogma when the tradition was practically void of Christology. Observation – by the time Mark wrote his Gospel the tradition contained obviously christological elements.[4] Inference – Mark did not originate the concept of the messianic secret.

It is not the case that analysis of Mark required Wrede's hypothesis. Rather his reconstruction of the history of earliest Christian dogma produced the hypothesis, and the hypothesis dominated his analysis of the Gospel of Mark.

## I

Wrede began his analysis of "the Messiah's self-concealment" (24–81) with a list of the Marcan passages indicating that the demons recognized Jesus as the Messiah,[5] from which – Wrede maintained – Mark's own view of the matter is clearly discernible (25). It was the demons, not the demon-possessed humans, who knew Jesus, and the demons' knowledge was supernatural knowledge, knowledge not of the man but of the one filled with the Spirit, the supernatural Son of God. The "unclean spirits" recognized the bearer of the Spirit as their enemy, their superior, whom they must obey. Thus Jesus' identity was, by its very nature, hidden from mere mortals, and the messianic secret was expressed not only by means of Jesus' commands to silence but also – and logically prior thereto – expressed implicitly in that only the demons knew who he really was (25).

Wrede's conclusions are thus also implicit at the outset, both on the nature of Mark's Christology and that the Messiah secret was not a part of the history of Jesus, for the historicality of the secrecy motif is of a piece with that of the demons, since it is they who provide the occasion for introducing the motif.

Having identified Mark's views on the relation of the demons to Jesus, Wrede then turned to the question, What motivated Mark – or one like him – to express this viewpoint and to emphasize it in the story of Jesus (33)? With that question Wrede presented Jesus' commands not to tell (34–6): (1) prohibitions to the demons (1:25, 34; 3:12), (2) prohibitions after (other) miracles (1:43–5; 5:43; 7:36; 8:26), (3) prohibitions after Peter's confession (8:30; 9:9), (4) Jesus' intention to preserve his incognito (7:24; 9:30f), (5) a prohibition not by Jesus himself (10:47f).

Wrede's observations are acute and his critique of explanations from the history of Jesus devastating. He concluded this part of his discussion by saying:

> Thus all accounts of Jesus' commands to silence which are placed before Peter's confession are shown – for more than one reason – to be incredible. That gives rise to the strong suspicion that the same is true of the few other instances. Mark 9:9 would in any case arouse such suspicion.... Furthermore that suspicion becomes certainty when Mark's own viewpoint is disclosed. For the explanation must lie in Mark's viewpoint if the history [of Jesus] fails to furnish it (53).

Wrede then (53–66) considered "related material" (omitted in English subtitle, 53), first asking whether the various expressions of Jesus' efforts towards privacy were part of the same secrecy motif, a question he left unanswered (55). Next he analysed the statements on the use of parables in 4:10–13, 33–4 (56–66). His conclusion here, much as in the case of the commands to silence, is that "The statement that the mystery of the kingdom of God has been given to the disciples ... together with its opposite gives very precise expression to the evangelist's viewpoint. It is incomprehensible that it should then be attributed to a source other than this viewpoint, to which the other material has been ascribed" (63).

The outcome of these discussions was not however to answer the question of what motivated "Mark or one like him", but to refute the false answers to that question which contemporary Jesus research had thought to give from the history of Jesus. Wrede's discussion of the Marcan text and its then current exegesis produced the conclusion that the idea of the messianic secret was not a part of Jesus' history but had its origin in the history of dogma (see 67). Throughout Wrede argued against the view that the Messiah secret had been a part of the actual history of Jesus,[6] and he seemed unaware that such argument is not the same as a pursuit of Mark's intention.

## II

The charge that Wrede read back into Mark his own view of the development of early Christology is also supported by his treatment of the command to silence following the transfiguration, Jesus' statement that the disciples were "to tell no one what they had seen, until the Son of man should have risen from the dead" (9:9).

One is struck by how much Wrede made of this command to silence while exerting so little effort at justifying that emphasis. He considered 9:9 the key text for understanding the messianic secret (67) but hardly bothered to try the key in the lock. Here is the place Wrede jumped over Mark into his own reconstruction of earliest Christian history, taking the reference to the resurrection as his springboard. He almost entirely neglected to assess how the statement functioned in its Marcan context. Rarely did he consider whether 9:9 was related to the predictions of the passion, although that is the Marcan setting of the passage (following the first prediction 8:31f and preceding its echo 9:12), and, when he did consider it, it was only in passing (83, 124). And although he noted the significance of Elijah as messianic forerunner (214), he seems to have felt no need to relate 9:9 to the closely following allusions to Elijah in 9:11–13. Nor, in considering the possibility Mark might have taken the transfiguration as a proleptic portrayal of the coming Messiah (225), did Wrede treat the proximity *in Mark* of the transfiguration (9:2–8) and 9:9.[7]

After tabulating the commands to secrecy Wrede noted that they were stereotyped in form and that a peculiarity of the command at 9:9 is its reference to the resurrection (37). It is this peculiarity which he took to express "the point of Mark's entire conception" (68) of the messianic secret (Jesus' messiahship concealed during his life and first disclosed at the resurrection), for "it is no more difficult to assume this idea frequently in Mark than to find it [only] once. And it is necessary to presuppose it everywhere, if the one instance is of the same kind as the others."[8] This is surely the key to Wrede's argument, whether or not it unlocks an understanding of the composition of the Gospel of Mark. Wrede's case requires the assumption that "the one instance is of the same kind as the others", the assumption that the several expressions of secrecy in Mark are articulations of a single unified viewpoint. And since that unity of viewpoint is not apparent in the Gospel of Mark, Wrede had to locate the origin of the concept prior to Mark. Yet despite its absence from the Gospel of Mark, Wrede held that unified viewpoint to be "the point of Mark's entire conception".

Wrede thought his interpretation of 9:9 was confirmed in the statement about the lamp under the bushel, "For there is nothing hid, except to be made manifest; nor is anything secret, except to come to light" (4:21f). This speaks clearly of concealment and disclosure; what it does *not* clearly say is precisely what Wrede's interpretation requires and what he therefore had to read into the Marcan text: "Rather the passage refers back [sc. to Mark 4:11] to the thought that secrets are communicated in the parables. For the time being only the disciples are recipients of this knowledge. But what they received they are later – let me clarify: *after the resurrection* – to disclose and publicize" (71). Wrede even admitted the point himself: "So far as I can see Mark did not really express these ideas in his Gospel. But he *cannot have held* any other viewpoint" (112). Thereafter Wrede referred to these ideas as Mark's view.[9]

It is important to see clearly the great advantages Wrede's historical reconstruction seemed to hold for the dynamics of his argument. He saw the force of this hypothesis in its ability to provide a single explanation of the phenomena: "The most forceful explanation has to be that one which presents a unified thought" (38). And Hans Jürgen Ebeling made the same point against Wrede's critics: "Up to now the force of his evidence defies all attempts to reduce the complex of his proof-texts or by enlarging the complex to generalize it and so to rob it of its force."[10] By locating the unified secrecy concept prior to Mark, Wrede could tolerate the incoherence he found by positing the coherence he required. He could attribute individual expressions of the concept as well as the articulation of the whole to Marcan editing and yet avoid the burden of showing "what the narrator in his own time wanted to say to his readers", for the concept, in Wrede's view, spoke with clarity and coherence at the time of its origin whereas by Mark's time the initial coherence had slackened and some expressions of the concept were but Marcan mannerisms. While the inconsistencies thus appear to be manageable on Wrede's hypothesis, they do not, as he claimed, require it. In fact the whole category, "inconsistency" among "the individual conceptions of the idea", is a product of Wrede's hypothesis, for they are labelled "inconsistencies" by reference to the hypothetical pre-Marcan unified secrecy concept. The intolerable inconsistency was between Wrede's hypothesis and the Marcan data.[11] Unity of concept is necessary to Wrede's hypothesis. When he and Ebeling claimed it as a strength of the hypothesis, they were turning a necessity into a virtue.

## III

The main weakness of Wrede's hypothesis, beyond internal structural faults, appeared only four years after the publication of his book. In 1905 Emil Wendling published his *Ur-Marcus*, in which on literary critical grounds[12] he attributed to Mark all the commands to silence except those at 1:25 and 1:44.[13] With that, Mark himself had to be given responsibility not only for articulating the messianic secret in his Gospel (so Wrede, 145) but also, it would seem, for originating the topic, and those "inconsistencies" which Wrede said could not be the work of a single individual would have to be accounted for as the work of that individual we call Mark.

Bultmann continued to treat the various expressions of secrecy in Mark as presenting a unified concept,[14] and he saw Martin Dibelius' characterization of the Gospel as solving the problem of inconsistencies: Mark's Gospel was "a book of secret epiphanies". Furthermore Bultmann held to Wrede's explanation of the messianic secret, that it served to veil the fact that belief in Jesus' messiahship arose first after faith in the resurrection (*idem*). Ebeling and Sjöberg showed the fallacy of that explanation: "Where in the Gospel of Mark are we to find that unmessianic tradition of Jesus' life which Mark, by means of the secrecy theory, wanted to reconcile with the belief that Jesus was Messiah during his lifetime?"[15] Hans Conzelmann is said to have got Bultmann's agreement on this issue by putting the matter in characteristically pointed brevity: If the messianic secret were a means for imposing a Christology on a non-christological tradition, then we should expect to find the commands to silence attached to non-christological material, whereas in fact their points of attachment are super-christological.

But Conzelmann's formula does not open up the whole truth, as analysis of the position of the commands will show, so that the unifying principle implicit in his dictum – to modify an already existing Christology – must also be classed as probandum, not as premise.

When we turn to the Marcan data, we recall that Wrede listed nine passages where Jesus commands silence: 1:25, 34, 44; 3:12; 5:43; 7:36; (*v.l.* 8:26); 8:30; 9:9 (plus the command at 10:48, which is not from Jesus). To put these data into perspective with the composition of Mark's Gospel as a whole, it should be noted that Jesus gave orders not to tell anyone else in only three of the thirteen miracle accounts in Mark and in none of the three exorcisms:

| EXORCISMS | | MIRACLES | | | |
|---|---|---|---|---|---|
| 1 | 1:21–8 | | 1 | 1:29–31 | Healing Peter's mother-in-law |
| 2 | 5:1–20 | + | 2 | 1:40–5 | Cleansing the leper |
| 3 | 9:14–27 | | 3 | 2:1–12 | Healing the paralytic |
| | | | 4 | 3:1–6 | Restoring the withered hand |
| | | | 5 | 4:35–41 | Calming the storm at sea |
| | | + | 6 | 5:21–4, 35–43 | Raising Jairus' daughter |
| | | | 7 | 5:25–34 | Stopping the haemorrhage |
| | | | 8 | 6:32–44 | Feeding the five thousand |
| | | | 9 | 6:45–52 | Walking on the water |
| | | + | 10 | 7:31–7 | Healing the deaf mute |
| | | | 11 | 8:1–10 | Feeding the four thousand |
| | | | 12 | 8:22–6 | The blind man at Bethsaida |
| | | | 13 | 10:46–52 | Bartimaeus receiving his sight |

The first command to silence is at 1:25, the man with the unclean spirit, where the literary form is exorcism. The command fits the form, in which it is the exorcist's potent word by which he overpowers the unclean spirit. "Be silent!" functions here just as does the similar command in the account of the stilling of the storm, 4:39: "Hush! Be silent!" That is, the command at 1:25 is *not* an expression of the messianic secret. It may be said to *become* that only in the Marcan interpretation some verses later, in the editorial statement at 1:34, "He did not permit the demons to speak because they knew him."

In this interpretative comment Mark has pulled the command from the exorcism into another language game, and it is only in that second semantic locus that the command expresses the messianic secret. In this first instance then the messianic secret is due to Mark: It is not in the pre-Marcan tradition. It is also worth noting that here Mark seems not to have altered the tradition.

The Gospel of Mark contains two other exorcism accounts, the Gerasene demoniac (5:1–20) and the son possessed from his childhood (9:14–27). In each case the demon recognized the exorcist. In the story of the Gerasene demoniac recognition is evident from the demon's action (running and kneeling before him, 5:6) and his address to Jesus, "Jesus, Son of the Most High God" (5:7), and in the second instance by action (convulsing the boy, 9:20) which included an outcry (9:26) but without any articulated address to Jesus – the demon was mute (9:17, 25). In both cases Jesus exerted his power over the demon by means of a command, but in neither is it a command to silence. Here again the tradition did not express the messianic secret and again Mark did not insert it into the tradition, even though the Gerasene demoniac addressed Jesus with a christological title, and despite the fact that there is an editorial aside inserted just after this word of address, I think inserted by Mark (5:8): "(For Jesus was already saying to him, 'Out, unclean spirit, come out of this man!')". Here then is a super-christological bit of tradition, where there is ground for thinking Mark inserted something but where he did *not* attach the messianic secret. Nor is there any appended interpretation as at 1:34.

As to exorcisms, therefore, it seems one must conclude that the messianic secret was neither in the traditional material nor inserted into it by Mark but occurs only in the Marcan interpretative summaries at 1:34 and 3:12.

Nor does point of attachment seem to offer greater promise as a unifying consideration when one turns from exorcisms to the other miracles. First of all, commands to silence are attached to so few of the miracles – in only three of 13 instances – that they can hardly have been intended to indicate concealment of all the miracles.[16]

Furthermore, in two of the three instances of commands to silence which are attached to miracles, it is expressly stated that the command was ignored. After the cleansing of the leper (1:45), the man went out and made the whole story public; he spread it far and wide until Jesus could no longer show himself in any town, but stayed outside in the open country. Even so people kept coming to him from all quarters. And at 7:36, after the healing of the deaf mute, Jesus forbade them to tell anyone, but the more he forbade it, the more they published it. In this connection it should also be noted that the exorcism account in chapter one concludes by saying that the news spread rapidly, and he was soon spoken of all over the district of Galilee (1:28).[17]

Are we to conclude then that it was Mark's intention to conceal only the exorcisms?[18] But we have just noted that the first editorial statement of the spread of Jesus' fame followed the first exorcism (at 1:28). At that point Mark made no separate category for exorcism, for what got notoriety was not the demon's knowledge of Jesus' true identity but the reaction of those who witnessed the exorcism. In this respect then Mark treated the exorcism like a healing miracle, as a demonstration of Jesus' power. The case is similar at the conclusion of the second exorcism (5:19f), where it is no longer a question of the demon but of the man of Gerasa, now restored, whom Jesus commanded, "Go home to your own folk and tell them what the Lord in his mercy has done for you." I think that statement is from the tradition and that Mark in the next verse modified the tradition only to say that the man told what *Jesus* had done for him. Thus in the second exorcism account Mark found and emphasized what he himself added to the first, an indication that word of Jesus' power spread. But surely the remaining exorcism (9:14–27) fits the view we have been schooled to accept, for is it not clear that Jesus concealed the exorcism by hastening to perform it before the witnesses arrived? "Jesus saw then that the crowd was closing in upon them, so he rebuked the unclean spirit" (9:25). Against this comforting observation two things need to be said. First, Wrede himself hesitated to claim for his concept the various expressions of a privacy motif (55). Withdrawal from the public belongs in the genre of mighty deeds,[19] so that I think we do better to respect Wrede's hesitation[20] rather than to ascribe the various privacy motifs to a Messiah secret complex.[21] The second difficulty is in the peculiar structure of the account itself, for after the exorcism we are told that the boy looked like a corpse; in fact many said, "He is dead." But Jesus took his hand and raised him to his feet, and he stood up (9:26f). Whether or not this is due to a combination of two originally distinct accounts,[22] the story as it now stands turns out to be a demonstration of power, like a healing miracle, and in the presence of witnesses. In his editing of the exorcisms Mark seems not to have distinguished them from other miracles but to have treated all miracles as demonstrations of Jesus' power, not as betrayals of his christological identity.

Hopes for clarity raised by Conzelmann's statement have so far been disappointed. Up to this point it has not seemed possible to unite the data under the rubric that commands to silence are attached to super-christological material. On the contrary, our analysis of Mark's editorial practice in the case of the first exorcism would seem to hold true generally: he has, in the main, left the tradition intact. Even if we leave out of consideration the four miracles which are not healings (stilling the storm 4:35–41, the two feedings 6:32–44; 8:1–10, and the walking on the water 6:45–52) twelve remain (classing exorcisms with other healings, as Mark seems to have done). Commands to silence occur with only three of them, and small as that proportion is, its force is almost completely neutralized by the same number of instances of editorial statements that Jesus' fame spread.[23]

Mark's concern for secrecy seems therefore to be located only within the new language game which he created out of the vocabulary of exorcism and expressed in his summaries. There the object of concealment is Jesus' christological identity (1:34; 3:11f) not his power. And that agrees with what we have seen of Mark's treatment of the exorcism accounts: he presents them in a class with healing miracles, as demonstrations of Jesus' power. Furthermore, the contrast between general notoriety and concealment of this one point, Jesus' true identity, is present even within the two Marcan summaries, as Kertelge has noted.[24]

Hypotheses heretofore advanced to unify the material have seemed inadequate. Wrede's case for a pre-Marcan unified concept was not convincing in itself, and then it was further undermined by the literary analysis which attributed the commands to silence to Marcan editing. Dibelius' concept of "secret epiphanies" may suffice for the healing miracles but not for the silencing of the demons in the Marcan summaries. And Conzelmann's thesis – attachment to super-christological material – though true as far as it goes, does not account for the bulk of the super-christological material in the tradition, for most of it is not buffered with efforts at concealment.

So far our considerations seem to be leading to the conclusion that the messianic secret concept, in anything like the sense it has borne in the history of the discussion since Wrede, is appropriate only for the two editorial passages in which Jesus forbade the demons to disclose his christological identity. At this point we need to turn to the other passages in Wrede's list.

## IV

The remaining instances where Jesus forbade disclosure are two, one after Peter's confession (8:30), the other on leaving the scene of the transfiguration (9:9). Our discussion of the other commands has not produced a basis on which to interpret these two, so we must try to interpret them from within their contexts. That procedure is both methodologically orthodox and intrinsically promising as well, since these two have as their context that part of the Gospel where Mark's intentions are most apparent, the central section (8:27—10:52) which Wellhausen once labelled "the gospel in the Gospel".

The central section begins with Peter's confession and Jesus' first prediction of his death, includes two more predictions of his death, and reaches its thematic conclusion with the statement, "The Son of man also came not to be served but to serve, and to give his life a ransom for many" (10:45). Immediately after Jesus's first prediction of his death there is a section on discipleship: "If any man would come after me, let him deny himself and take up his cross and follow me. For whoever would save his life will lose it; and whoever loses his life for my sake and the gospel's will save it. For what does it profit a man, to gain the whole world and forfeit his life? For what can a man give in return for his life? For whoever is ashamed of me and of my words in this adulterous and sinful generation, of him will the Son of man also be ashamed, when he comes in the glory of his Father with the holy angels" (8:34–8). Thus at the start of the central section is stated the contrapuntal theme which governs it all, Jesus going steadfastly to his death as a ransom for many while the disciples tag along, grasping, anxious, petty, utterly blind to the pastoral obligations of discipleship. The central section contains pre-Marcan material and some pre-Marcan arrangement of material,[25] but is clear that Mark has used the material[26] to create the powerful impression, to show by negation what is required of disciples. Here is where we find the remaining two commands to silence.

In discussing the commands to silence we have been using Wrede's distinction based on the material to which the commands pertained, exorcisms and other healing miracles. Formal analysis produces the same two-fold classification. Commands to demons echo the form of exorcism but commands following other healings do not. Demons are "rebuked" (*epitīmān*) while witnesses to healings are "ordered" (*diastellesthai*) to silence. Demons are forbidden to disclose "him", while witnesses to healings are enjoined against telling what they saw. In the exorcism form rebuke follows a christological title, while in the other form the command follows a healing miracle. Jesus' two commands to silence in the central section (8:30; 9:9) fit one in each of the two forms. At 8:30 rebuke follows a christological title addressed to Jesus, and what "they" are forbidden is "to tell about him". At 9:9 they are "ordered" to tell no one what they saw. However 9:9, in contrast to other instances of command (*diastellesthai*), follows a christological title, the voice from the cloud in the transfiguration scene: "This is my beloved Son . . .".

After Jesus had predicted his death and resurrection Peter rebuked him, whereupon (8:33) Jesus rebuked Peter, called him Satan, told him to get behind him, and explained this by saying "You think as men think, not as God thinks". Here at 8:33 interpretation manages fairly well: in opposing the crucifixion which is part of God's will (*dei*, 8:31), Peter had set himself against God and for that received the rebuke he was due. But why then are "they" rebuked and silenced at 8:30 following the confession of Jesus as the Christ? At that point neither Peter nor the disciples had voiced any heretical positive thinking. Nor was the Christology in error; on the contrary Peter's confession was orthodox. (The same should be said also about the titles the demons used.) Nor can one say the disciples are here declared to be demonic; the Satan statement a few verses later did not refer to supernatural knowledge the demons had of Jesus' identity, but referred to an attempt to thwart the divine will. The point of contact between the disciples and the demons would seem to be that each knew Jesus' true identity and stated it, whereupon Jesus commanded silence on that topic. The Christology was accurate but it was not to be expressed. (To this extent 8:30 is like the two editorial references to silencing the demons, 1:34; 3:11f).

I think Mark did not consider Peter's confession the high point of the Gospel – in the positive sense that phrase usually has in this connection, but that Mark had Jesus repudiate the disciples' confession of his identity because it was Christology separated from the theology of Jesus' death.[27] Whether Mark added Peter's attempt to persuade Jesus to avoid the cross or found it already in the tradition, it was in reference to this that Mark inserted the command to silence at 8:30. This interpretation explains the present context and agrees with what Mark emphasized throughout the central section of his Gospel: Jesus was going to his divinely ordained death "as a ransom for many" (10:45) while the disciples "followed" with an utter lack of comprehension which mocked the meaning of "following after".

In the central section Mark interpreted Jesus' death, an interpretation moving not in christological abstractions but directed towards concretion in discipleship, the issue of living one's life in a way commensurate with understanding one's reality from the theological interpretation of Jesus' death. Since Wrede, the hermeneutical approach to all these passages has been held to be primarily christological, how to think the thoughts of faith; but taken in its context 8:30 is differently aimed, on discipleship, how to live the life of faith. (In this respect 8:30 differs from 1:34; 3:12.)

This view of 8:30 is implicit in a currently popular interpretation of the secrecy motifs which moves in the tow of Georgi's book on Second Corinthians[28] and affirms Ebeling's and Sjöberg's criticism of Wrede, namely, that the Gospel of Mark furnishes us no evidence for the existence of a non-christological tradition onto which Mark might have wanted to impose a Christology. In this interpretation Mark's historical moment, far from being void of Christology, included a miracle-worker (*theios anēr*) Christology with a complementary Christian self-understanding, and Mark's aim was to correct that Christology – together with the view of discipleship implicit in it – by means of the theology of the cross. Nevertheless, attractive as it is, that *theios anēr* explanation of the Marcan commands to silence has the fundamental weakness that it presupposes what it has not shown (and what has been rejected above), the unity of the several expressions of secrecy in the Gospel of Mark, for only on that assumption can it hope to focus the commands sharply against the miracles. Failing that, one must, I think, seek the meaning of 8:30 within its own context, the central section of Mark's Gospel, and perhaps be content with the more general explanation that Mark was motivated by a concern for living the Christian life on the pattern of Jesus who gave himself for others.

In any case this much, I think, is clear: at 8:30 Mark's primary concern was discipleship, not Christology. Interpretation of 8:30 does not, however, necessarily clarify the other commands to silence, and 9:9 is yet to be considered. I think interpretation of 9:9 should begin – in accord with Wrede's principles – by trying seriously to make sense of the statement within its Marcan context rather than – as Wrede did – by taking one's point of departure outside the Gospel of Mark in a hypothetical reconstruction of the history of earliest Christian thought.

The first half of 9:9 is in form like the commands attached to miracles, but then the command is qualified by the statement, "until the Son of man had risen from the dead". Wrede knew all about this, but after testing his argument I feel more like the disciples, who "discussed among themselves what this 'rising from the dead' could mean" (9:10). The *New English Bible* is right to put "rising from the dead" in quotation marks; that is the force of the article before the words. It is not the concept of resurrection which was perplexing but why Jesus should refer to it in that context.

Even among those who reject Wrede's reconstruction, 9:9 is often taken to mean that Christological understanding of Jesus came with the resurrection faith. That is understandable both as a religious insight and as a critical historian's view of earliest Christianity, but it is by no means apparent that Mark meant it that way.

And if he had, how should one understand what follows the command to silence and the disciples' puzzling over why Jesus spoke of the rising from the dead? Why did Mark put 9:11–13 here? The verses are about the Malachi prophecy of the eschatological coming of Elijah, here an allusion to John the Baptist, but why here?

A connection between verses 11–13 and 9–10 is not obvious; agreed. The passage itself does not move smoothly; agreed. Wernle and Bultmann thought verse 12b was a copyist's insertion from

Matthew and so not originally in Mark; I disagree. For all its awkwardness the passage makes sense as it is: it reasserts the theme of Mark's central section, and at verse 12b in the very words of the preceding prediction of the passion: "Yet how is it that the scriptures say of the Son of man that he is to endure great sufferings and be treated with contempt?" According to the Malachi prophecy Elijah's eschatological function was "to set everything right" (Mark 9:12a) "before the great and terrible day of the Lord" (Mal. 4:5f). That prediction, in the present Marcan context, poses a theological problem: how is it that the Son of Man "is to endure great sufferings and be treated with contempt" *after* Elijah has come and "set everything right"? Verse 12b speaks to that problem[29] and is therefore integral to Mark's use of the passage here and thus a part of the original text of Mark, not an interpolation. Here the Malachi prophecy is historicized in the fate of John the Baptist, and John is set in parallel to Jesus in that they both were put to death – in both cases, "as it was written"! Though I see no clear continuity of thought from 9:9f to verses 11–13, the sequence is in Mark, and I think that Mark created it,[30] whether he also constructed verses 11–13[31] or only modified them.[32] If Mark put verses 11–13 after 9–10, then it appears that Mark has related the command to silence at 9:9 to Jesus' death just as he did at 8:30. References to the death of the Son of Man belong in chapters 8—10. But why John the Baptist?

A possible answer is this: the Christians were obviously engaged in a christological apologetic and polemic against those disciples of John the Baptist who maintained that he, as Elijah, was the last herald before the coming of God (Luke 1:16f, 76) and as such the "messianic" figure *par excellence.* This conflict began early enough to have left its mark in Q and must have continued for some time, since it appears in the Fourth Gospel and in material peculiar to Matthew or Luke, that is, not derivative from Mark, and therefore not just a literary topic. The Christian polemic in various ways subjected John to Jesus, showing that though John was first, Jesus was greater. One way to do this was to grant the relation of John to Elijah but to modify that Malachi prophecy to make Elijah/John the forerunner of the Messiah, Jesus, rather than of God himself. But that is not the line taken in Mark 9:11–13. Here the problem posed by the priority of John/Elijah is not that of competing christological identities; the question is rather, "Yet how is it that the scriptures say of the Son of man that he is to endure great sufferings and be treated with contempt?" At 8:30 Mark has silenced

Christology when separated from the crucifixion; here he has repudiated a Christian christological polemic against the Baptist's followers and in its place has tried to take over the significance of the Baptist rather than nullify it with christological superiority.

"The messianic secret" – if that term may properly still be used – is a Marcan motif, not in the pre-Marcan tradition nor even latent within it, for while Mark plundered the traditional exorcism accounts to express concealment of Jesus' identity, he so radically altered the meaning that it was not an extension of the tradition but something new. The traditions also furnished him certain privacy motifs[33] which he may have extended, for example, to private instruction of the disciples,[34] but a privacy motif prior to Mark requires no assumption of a messianic secret, since the motif is sufficiently explained as belonging to the genre of healing miracles.

Furthermore, it is not apparent that Mark combined the several privacy expressions into an articulation of the course of development of christological dogma. I expect this interpretation will be met with opposition, among other things, on the grounds cited above from Ebeling: it seems to atomize the material and so lacks the appealing tidiness of a unified explanation. Wrede clearly saw the difficulty of unifying the several motifs at the point of Mark's composition of the Gospel and so located the unified concept prior to Mark, but although literary criticism showed that move to be without sufficient warrant, the consequences of that criticism have been largely overlooked, with the result that what Wrede rejected – a discernible unity of concept at Mark's level – has been taken as Wrede's probated legacy. I think Mark did correlate some of the topics in this discussion but not under the principle of "the messianic secret", that is, not around the history of dogma issue of the development of Christology nor on a preoccupation with the historical distinction between Jesus' "then" and Mark's "now". I think Mark related the demons' knowledge and the disciples' ignorance as a means for insisting on relating Christology and the theology of the cross in order to emphasize the pastoral aspects of discipleship, that with that he may have correlated the humane exercise of the Son of Man's authority[35] and a reinterpretation of the relation of Jesus and John the Baptist. In these matters, as well as in some others, Mark took a position over against those who quibble over christological technicalities (scribes, Pharisees, and – disciples) to emphasize the point that disciples – those who "follow after" – are to follow him who gave himself for others.

## NOTES

1 215–17; Acts 2:36; Rom. 1:4; Phil. 2:6ff; the meaning of parousia: "coming", not "second coming".

2 228f: "Concealment presupposes something to be concealed."

3 E.g., 228–36.

4 Wrede's most frequent examples were Jesus' triumphal entry into Jerusalem and his answer to the high priest, e.g., 70, 239, although he also noted miracles without commands to silence and messianic address without rebuke, 36, 70.

5 Mark 1:23–5, 34; 3:11f, 5:6f; 9:20.

6 See e.g., 227.

7 He did refer to the connection of 9:9 and the transfiguration in arguing against the historicity of 9:9, p. 53.

8 69, cf. 38, 48, 67f.

9 E.g., 72, 165, 176, 178.

10 Ebeling, 1939, 114.

11 See Schweitzer, 1954, 341 on the triumphal entry and Jesus' reply to the high priest: "The real point is that Wrede cannot bring these two passages within the lines of the theory of secrecy...."

12 *Ur-Marcus. Versuch einer Wiederherstellung der ältesten Mitteilungen über das Leben Jesu* (Tübingen: J. C. B. Mohr [Paul Siebeck], 1905). Detailed in his *Die Entstehung des Marcus-Evangeliums* (Tübingen: J. C. B. Mohr [Paul Siebeck], 1908).

13 Rudolf Bultmann then decided that all but 1:25 were Marcan. See *Die Geschichte der synoptischen Tradition* (Göttingen: Vandenhoeck & Ruprecht, 1921, 1957[3]). The English translation is not reliable.

14 Ibid., 371.

15 Sjöberg, 1955, 115; so already Ebeling, 60: "The tradition is already interpreted, christologically interpreted, tradition." Cf. 16: "Epiphany tradition is thus the primary substance of the tradition."

16 The view that a few commands to silence were intended to conceal a greater number of miriacles would seem to gain in force if the few commands were attached one to each of several collections of miracles, thereby indicating the concealment of all the miracles in each collection, or strategically placed within a single collection of miracles with the same effect. Keck, Georgi, Achtemeier, and others have recently defended the view that Mark made use of collections of miracles, and in Achtemeier's reconstruction, two commands to silence are strategically placed. But in this application that line of argument is not pure gain; it introduces its own difficulties. If the commands to silence were in the presumed pre-Marcan collection(s), their inclusive function – to conceal all miracles in the collection – would cease when Mark broke up the collection(s) but did not repeat the commands when he distributed the miracles in his Gospel, so that one would face the same problem which Wrede thought to avoid by positing a unified expression of a unified concept only prior to Mark. And if it was Mark who added the commands to the collection, but then did not carry out the concealment motif when he

distributed the miracle collection(s) in composing his Gospel, what Wrede called "Mark's own viewpoint" would apply to notations Mark made in his source document(s) but did not see fit to spread over his Gospel, so that from the time Mark worked over his source(s) to the time he composed his Gospel, his intention in the former case would have become only a mannerism in the latter. Thus even on the assumption that Mark used an earlier miracle source(s), the point of attachment of the commands to silence does not provide a hermeneutical approach to the composition of the Gospel of Mark. See Leander Keck, "Mark 3:7–12 and Mark's Christology", *JBL*, 84 (1965) 341–58; Dieter Georgi, a paper read at the meeting of the Northeastern Section, SBL, 31 March 1971; Paul Achtemeier, "Toward the Isolation of Pre-Markan Miracle Catenae", *JBL*, (1970) 89:265–91.

17. NB: all three statements on the spread of Jesus' fame are widely held to be Mark's own editorial additions.

18 The violation of commands to silence is so pronounced that several – e.g. Ebeling and Luz – have categorized the material under two headings, saying the intent was to conceal in the case of silencing the demons but that in the case of healing miracles Mark wanted to show that Jesus' power was irrepressibly evident – so already Wendling, *Entstehung*, 17, 53, 60, 80. Then Dibelius' dictum on "secret epiphanies" might apply, but only to the healing miracles, not to the silencing of the demons.

19 Bultmann, 227, 229, 239 and n. 4.

20 So Bultmann, 239.

21 As has been done by Luz, Strecker [see the essays here] and Kertelge, 1970.

22 Bultmann, 241.

23 Sjöberg is right that violation of the commands to silence is just as characteristic of Mark's presentation as are the commands themselves, 116.

24 Page 32.

25 Kuhn, 1971.

26 Ibid., 181ff.

27 So Weeden, 1971. See also 1:34; 3:11f.

28 *Die Gegner des Paulus im 2. Korintherbrief* (WMANT, Neukirchen-Vluyn; Neukirchener, 1964).

29 So Weisse, 1838, cited by Wellhausen.

30 So Wendling, *Entstehung*, 211; Dibelius, 1934, 226f.

31 Taylor, 1952, 83; Johannes Schreiber, *Theologie des Vertrauens* (Hamburg: Furche-Verlag, 1967), 28.

32 Sjöberg, 162 n. 2.

33 E.g., the performance of healing miracles apart from the public, 5:40; 7:33; 8:23.

34 See 7:24, 10:10, which Wrede, 136, 146, considered examples of Marcan mannerism.

35 To forgive sins, 2:10: to humanize the sabbath, 2:27f; cf. 10:45.

# 8
# *The Messianic Secret in Mark*[*1]

JAMES D. G. DUNN

William Wrede's *Das Messiasgeheimnis in den Evangelien* (1901) marked a turning point of considerable importance in the study of the Gospels inasmuch as Wrede was really the first to recognize and appreciate the theological nature of the synoptics. His specific thesis (that the messianic secret motif in Mark has a theological rather than a historical origin) has "mark"edly influenced the researches of those who came after him, to such an extent that it is often taken for granted, a "given" in the investigation of new propositions and theses. His own statement of the thesis has not escaped criticism and refinement, of course, but his main conclusion still stands as proven for the majority of continental scholars.

Wrede points first to the commands with which Jesus silences the messianic confessions of the demons (1:23–5, 34; 3:11f; cf.5:6f; 9:20). Since the various explanations offered for the possessed individual's knowledge are unsatisfactory, we must recognize a legendary development in the tradition. When other commands to silence are also taken into consideration – to those healed miraculously (1:43–5; 5:43; 7:36; 8:26), the disciples after Peter's confession (8:30) and after the transfiguration (9:9) – as also the intention of Jesus to remain hidden (7:24; 9:30f) and the command addressed by the crowd to Bartimaeus to be silent (10:47f), it becomes evident that what is being thus guarded is the messianic secret. He goes on to cite other evidence, the most notable of which are the private instructions which Jesus gives to the disciples (4:34; 7:17–23; 9:28f; 8:31; 9:31; 10:32–4; 13:3ff) and the saying about parabolic teaching (4:10–13). On the basis of this evidence Wrede delivers his judgement – namely that for Mark there is no historical motif in question; rather the idea of the messianic secret is a wholly theological conception. The key is Mark

* First published in *Tyn Bul* 21 (1970) 92–117. The text used here is a slightly abbreviated version first published in the *TSF Bulletin* (1974), in which the footnotes have been considerably reduced.

9:9, when Peter, James and John are commanded not to speak of what they had seen until the Son of Man should have risen from the dead. Jesus' messiahship is and must be a secret. Only the inner circle can be let into the secret. But with the resurrection comes the relevation to all. In short, the whole is a theological construction. Jesus did not in fact claim to be Messiah during his ministry, and it was not until after the resurrection that his messianic status was affirmed by the Christian community. The messianic secret is nothing other than the attempt made by Mark to account for the absence of messianic claims by Jesus himself.

## I

An analysis of Wrede's thesis reveals three principal strands: first, the isolation of a distinct motif in Mark which can be called the "messianic secret"; second, the argument that certain elements of that motif, noticeably the exorcisms, are non-historical, leading to the conclusion that the whole motif is the construction of Christian or Marcan theology (the more recent rise of form criticism has, of course, given more depth and consistency to this argument); third, as the *raison d'être*, the complementary argument that belief in Jesus as Messiah was an Easter faith and that the messianic secret results from an attempt to read back messiahship into the life of Jesus.

(1) If this is a fair representation of Wrede's argument it seems to me to be open to several major criticisms. The first of these is that Wrede has narrowed the scope of the secrecy motif too much. I strongly question whether the silences commanded by Jesus in connection with the healing miracles can adequately be brought under the category of *messianic* secret. What is there about the healings that cannot be understood before the cross and resurrection which is not *publicly* demonstrated in, for example, the healing of the paralytic before the scribes in chap. 2, or the healing of the man with the withered arm in the synagogue in chap. 3? What is there about the healing miracles which particularly marks out Jesus as Messiah? According to Mark not one of the miracles performed publicly led the spectators to conclude that Jesus was the Messiah (though see below, pp. 122ff), while several passages indicate that their reaction was often completely different. The people of Nazareth saw only the carpenter, the member of a well-known local family, despite the public knowledge of his miracles (6:1–6). Herod and others thought he might be John the Baptist resurrected, or Elijah

or another prophet (6:14f; 8:28). The Pharisees judged him to be possessed by Beelzebub (3:22). Moreover, the only recipient of Jesus' healing who hails him in messianic terms (10:46ff) is *not* silenced by Jesus. So just what secret was being safeguarded by those commands to silence?

The attempt to bring all the healing miracle commands to silence under the heading of "messianic secret" fails to carry conviction. Despite Wrede's belief that only one explanation must be applied to the so-called secrecy passages, it is highly probable that in different situations there was a variety of motives operative – and particularly in Jesus' dealings with the sick: e.g. desire for privacy and concern for the well-being of the individual being cured (cf. 1:44; 5:40; 7:33; 8:22, 26; 9:25), as well as the wish to discourage misleading ideas about himself from gaining fresh currency, and perhaps the strong sense that his destiny was completely in the hands of God. In this connection it is worth noting that there are grounds for recognizing 1:21–45 as a pre-Marcan block of material in whose construction one of the determining motifs was the way in which excessive publicity resulted in increasing restriction on Jesus' movement and ministry (Capernaum, country towns, desert areas – 1:21, 38, 45).

I question also whether the saying about the use of parables can be counted as part of the evidence for the messianic secret. In Mark 4:11 what Jesus says is that parables conceal the mystery of the *Kingdom* from *hoi exō* – and while I would agree that the mystery of the Kingdom is closely related to the historical status and ministry of Jesus, it is not to be wholly identified with the messiahship of the earthly Jesus. Besides, both 4:11 ("to those who are outside *everything* comes in parables") and 4:34 ("he would not speak to them except in parables") indicate that it was his *whole* ministry of word and deed which had this parabolic effect – and his whole ministry cannot be contained within the bounds of the messianic secret. In 7:17, for example, the parable whose explanation he gives to the disciples in private is his teaching about inward cleanliness. One should also note that if 4:11 (the illumination of the disciples) is interpreted in terms of the messianic secret it at once comes into conflict with passages like 9:32 (the incomprehension of the disciples).

Turning to this latter theme, the obtuseness of the disciples, which is often cited as an important element in Mark's theology of the messianic secret, even this cannot be contained within its scope. I would be prepared to admit the instance of the disciples' astonishment and hardness of heart at the stilling of the storm as part of the messianic secret (6:51–2). For I certainly see messianic significance in the feeding of the five thousand, although I am not so sure that Mark wished to bring out that significance, and Mark does specifically say that the disciples were dumbfounded "because they had not seen what the miracle of the loaves meant" (Jerusalem Bible – *ou gar sunēkan epi tois artois*). For the same reason I can see the justification for including the disciples' misunderstanding over the saying about the yeast of the Pharisees and of Herod with the messianic secret, although the passage is a difficult one. For once again their obtuseness is underlined by a reference to the feeding of the five thousand and the feeding of the four thousand, and the pericope ends with the words of Jesus *oupō suniete*; but it is impossible to bring 10:10 under the messianic secret – for what the disciples enquire of him in private (*eis tēn oikian*) is the meaning of his saying about divorce and marriage – hardly a distinctively messianic theme.

Bearing in mind this diversity in the situations which demonstrate the disciples' obtuseness, it is more plausible to recognize in the motif a historical reminiscence of the very natural and unexceptional slowness of unlettered men whose rigid and closed system of thought made it difficult for them to adjust to new teaching. It was not simply the difficulty of coping with new information, but the impossibility of trying to assimilate that new information into a system of thought and reference which had no place for such information. The situation which would cause a computer either to admit defeat or to explode, caused only confusion and incomprehension on the part of the disciples. Such a situation can be resolved only by a conversion of mind, something which by all accounts did not happen to the disciples till the gift of the Spirit after Jesus' resurrection. To go to the other extreme and attribute the motif to a Marcan polemic against the disciples is certainly uncalled for.

I rather suspect that Wrede was misled by taking the exorcisms as his starting-point. It was natural that a nineteenth/twentieth-century man should fasten on to these incidents which were to him among the most bizarre and incredible, and which for that very reason gave him immediate access to the theological viewpoint of the primitive Church – that is, to the way the primitive Church had viewed and worked over the historical facts. No psychological argument could explain how, for example, the Gerasene demoniac came to hail Jesus as Son of the Most High God, and recourse to a supernatural explanation was unacceptable. Therefore, Wrede concluded, we are in the presence of a legendary development in the tradition which leads us straight into the heart of the messianic secret. Leaving aside the issue of demon-possession and the possibility of "supernatural" knowledge, which I personally hold to be a far more open question than Wrede allowed, it still seems to me that Wrede's approach was methodologically suspect. For the exorcism narratives would not stand out so prominently in Mark's time. The fact is that in their manner of presentation they accord by and large with the standard pattern of exorcism stories, even to the extent of the demon using the name of the exorcist and the exorcist commanding the demon to silence, and the knowledgeable reader of Mark's Gospel would see nothing out of the ordinary in Jesus' response to the demon's cry in Mark 1:25 – *phimōthēti kai exelthe ex autou.* I recognize that there is weight to the counter-argument that *Mark* understood the injunction to silence in this first exorcism in terms of 1:34 and 3:11f, which could well be taken to indicate that demoniacs regularly hailed him as Son of God and that Jesus' usual response was a strong warning that they should not make him known. But if Mark was trying to "get over" to his readers the message of the messianic secret the first exorcism would give no indication of it to his readers. In fact, the distinctive messianic secret motif only appears in these two summary statements, and there are no commands to silence in any of the other exorcisms where the narrative goes into any detail (5:1–20; 7:24–30; 9:14–29). I question therefore whether Wrede was right to single out the exorcisms as the decisive clue to the meaning of the secrecy theme in Mark.

(2) If the first criticism puts a question mark against Wrede's isolation of a specifically *messianic* secret, my second puts a question mark against his calling the motif "messianic *secret*". For it appears to me that Wrede did not give sufficient weight to what might be called a counter-balancing publicity-revelation theme which seems frequently to run directly counter to the secrecy motif. After the first exorcism Mark says "his reputation spread everywhere (*pantachou*) through all (*holēn*) the surrounding Galilean countryside" (1:28). After the healing of the leper we are told that the leper started talking about it freely and telling the story everywhere, so that Jesus could no longer go openly into any town but had to stay outside in places where nobody lived. Even so, people from all around came to him (1:45). On another occasion Mark says "once again such a crowd collected that they could not even have a meal" (3:20). And far from commanding him to be silent Jesus orders the Gerasene demoniac, now cured, to "go home to your people and tell them all that the

Lord in his mercy has done for you" (5:19f). In Nazareth they certainly knew all about his miracles, (6:2–3), and so remarkable and public were they that all sorts of rumours were current about him (6:14ff; 8:28). The feeding of the five thousand was the result of an attempted escape to seclusion on the part of Jesus and his disciples, because "there were so many coming and going that the apostles had no time to eat" (6:31). And in the region of Tyre and Sidon he entered a house (*eis oikian*) and did not want anyone to know it; but it was impossible for him to be concealed (7:24). To cite but one other instance, it is certainly remarkable, if we believe that the messianic secret motif decisively shaped the material, that Bartimaeus should be allowed to be depicted as twice loudly hailing Jesus as Son of David – *and* Jesus neither rebukes him nor tells him to be silent (10:46ff)! In view of the messianic significance of the title Son of David (12:35–7a) it is surely quite inadequate to dismiss this pericope as having nothing to do with the theory of the messianic secret, as Wrede and those who follow him do.

So far as the messianic secret is concerned the publicity theme is most noticeable in the contexts where one would expect withdrawal and silence. In the healing of the paralytic Mark alone says that the proof of the miracle – his rising and walking off – happened "in full view of them all" (2:12 NEB). And in the case of the man with the withered arm, far from performing the miracle privately, Jesus commands him *egeire eis to meson* and there, having first drawn all eyes upon him, effects the healing (3:3ff). It is true that there is a secrecy, or better, privacy motif in some of the healings (5:37ff; 7:31–7; 8:22–6). But the woman with the haemorrhage is healed in the crowd and it is Jesus himself who draws attention to a cure which no one else had noticed. And Bartimaeus is healed in full view of the crowd. Nor surely was Mark naive enough to impose a messianic secret motif on a story like the raising of Jairus' daughter. How could the raising of a dead girl to life be kept silent when the mourning had already begun? And why is it on several occasions after Jesus gives a strict command to silence that Mark immediately goes on to tell how the news was broadcast far and wide (1:25–8, 43–5; 7:36f)? If the messianic secret motif was added to explain why Jesus was not recognized as Messiah, and part of that motif is the command to demons and men not to tell of their cures, I am at a loss to understand what Mark was trying to achieve by adding or at least retaining the publicity sequel. For the whole point of these passages is that the secret commanded was *not* kept. The commands to silence failed, and so the so-called attempt to keep his messiahship secret also failed.

If the messianic secret was a Marcan theory, then these publicity passages are the *reductio ad absurdum* of that theory. This publicity motif shows that at most we can speak of a messianic *misunderstanding*, but hardly of a messianic *secret*.

There is also a very prominent theme of revelation which should not be ignored. I will not enlarge upon it but simply call attention to its various facets – the authoritative claims made by the Marcan Jesus for himself: to forgive sins, no less (2:10); to have a mission to call (*kalesai*) sinners (2:17); to be sovereign (*kurios*) over the sabbath (2:28); to be the one who binds the strong man (Satan) and ransacks his house (3:27); that loyalty to *him* will be the yardstick of judgement in the parousia (8:38). Again there is the teaching Jesus gives to his disciples in private about the true nature of his messiahship (8:31–3; 9:31–2; 10:32–4, 45; 14:22–5). Schweizer justifiably notes the concern with which Jesus brings God's mystery to men, especially the disciples (4:34; 7:17–23; 8:15–21, 27–33; 9:30–2; 10:32–4; cf. 5:37; 9:2; 13:3f).[1] Finally, one might call attention to such passages as the Parable of the Wicked Tenants, where the Marcan Jesus specifically claims a special relation of sonship and where Mark tells us that the priests and lawyers recognized that the parable was aimed at them (12:12); or again to the Bartimaeus episode where Jesus is twice hailed as Son of David (10:47f) and to 15:39 where the centurion confesses that the *dead* Jesus was truly a or the Son of God. A theory of the messianic secret which does not take account of these other themes which are just as prominent will inevitably give a distorted picture both of the Marcan Jesus and of the Marcan theology.

(3) My third criticism of Wrede's thesis is that it does not give sufficient weight to the element of historicity which is firmly attached to the motif of the messianic secret. As I have already indicated, Wrede believed that Jesus did not claim to be Messiah during his life and that all messianic elements were superimposed upon the tradition. But in my opinion there are several incidents whose historicity it is almost impossible to dismiss and whose central significance has definite messianic overtones – a significance which must have been known to and intended by Jesus.

I think first of the feeding of the five thousand. As John O'Neill observes, "we may suppose that some extraordinary event will lie behind such a miraculous narrative ... it remains true that if Jesus did preside at a communal meal in the desert places of Galilee and Judaea, this would have had peculiar significance to his contemporaries. They would perhaps remember that Moses by praying to God was able to feed the people with manna and quail in the desert; they would perhaps be reminded of the promise that the desert would again be fruitful; and they would think of the shepherd King as they were given food in the barren places (cf. *Pss. Sol.* xvii. 45). The Qumran desert community placed great emphasis on communal meals, and looked forward to the time when the Messiah of Aaron would preside and the Messiah of Israel, whom God had begotten among them, would come (IQSa ii. 11–22)."[2]

Even more to the point is the evidence of John 6:15 that the crowd intended to "come and seize Jesus to proclaim him king". C. H. Dodd argues, convincingly I think, for the historicity of John 6:14f. Most noticeable is the otherwise very odd use of *ēnangkasen* in Mark 6:45 – Jesus had to force the disciples to put out into a difficult sea. The two independent traditions interlock and together provide a very coherent picture. The crowd see the messianic significance of Jesus' action and are so carried away on a wave of mass enthusiasm that they attempt to make him king by acclamation. The disciples themselves are caught up in the excitement, and Jesus in order to forestall the move has first to force the disciples to embark by themselves on an uninviting lake. Only then is he able to turn to the crowd and with the voice of authority to dismiss them (*apoluein*). He then goes off immediately by himself into the hills to pray – and it is perhaps significant that Mark only mentions Jesus praying three times, and that on each of the other occasions the implication is that he resorted to prayer because of temptation – temptation at the time of his early success to remain where he was so popular (1:35, 38); temptation in Gethsemane (14:35f). So in 6:46 there is the implication that Jesus was tempted to give way to the crowd's demands – to be the Messiah of popular conception and popular appeal, and that he fled to the silence and loneliness of the hills that quiet communion with his Father might strengthen his conviction concerning the nature of his mission and messiahship. Whether Mark was aware of the messianic significance of the story he recorded it is hard to say; but I would strongly maintain that that significance is inherent in the historical incident he records.

I think secondly of Peter's confession in Mark 8:27ff, a passage which caused Wrede not a little difficulty. Points in favour of the substantial authenticity of the pericope are: the specification and location of the place of confession (none of the traditional resurrection appearances to the twelve took place so far north), the unique appearance of the title *Christos* addressed to Jesus by a disciple, the evidence that Jesus was *Pneumatiker*, and the total improbability of the primitive Church calling Peter "Satan". Nor should we ignore the otherwise surprising insertion *kai idōn tous mathētas autou* in v. 33a, which has the ring of an authentic reminiscence, and the Jewish character of v. 33. Grundmann also calls attention to the thrice repeated *epitimān* and to the *ērxato didaskein* which is not the normal Marcan semitism but indicates a particular point of time at which for the first time the repeated teaching referred to by the *didaskein* received a concrete content.[3]

As for the passage as a whole, and without being able to go into detail, I may say that I am not convinced by the arguments which attribute the connection between 8:27–30 and 8:31ff solely to Marcan theology. It is unquestionable in my opinion that Jesus saw (or at least came to see) his mission in terms of suffering, and entirely probable that he should begin to explain this to his most intimate followers at some stage in his ministry. Nor do I feel it necessary to attribute v. 30 – the command to silence – to the hand of an interpolator. For it is not the Christ of Easter whom Peter confesses, or else why is he rebuked? And if it is the Christ of Jewish hope and popular expectation whom Peter hails – as the rebuke requires – a pre-Easter origin cannot so readily be denied to the confession. Here again then is an account whose historical substance is of irreducible messianic significance.

The third incident in which I believe historicity and messianic significance go together is the entry into Jerusalem. On the score of historicity Vincent Taylor points to "the local expressions at the beginning, the vivid character of the account ... the description of what happened, the restrained nature of the acclamation, and the strange manner in which the account breaks off without any suggestion of a 'triumphal entry' (as in Matt.)".[4] One might also note that the actions and shouts of those with Jesus create an impression of authenticity, because though they conform in a general way to Zech. 9:9 they include details which are neither necessary nor even particularly appropriate – a fact which makes it unlikely that the narrative is a construction of the primitive Church. Specially worthy of comment is the appearance of *hōsanna*, which is firmly embedded in the synoptic tradition, and also in John's account, but which appears nowhere else in the NT – a strong indication of authenticity. I therefore find Taylor's conclusion wholly justified: "These characteristics suggest the eyewitness rather than the artist."[5]

As for messianic significance, we may note in the words of D. E. Nineham, "It is difficult to see why Jesus sent for the colt and entered the city on it unless he intended to make clear the fact of his Messiahship. Pilgrims normally entered Jerusalem on foot, so, as the story stands, the fact that Jesus deliberately procured and rode an ass makes it impossible to think of him as simply a passive figure in a demonstration which was none of his doing."[6]

The messianic associations of the Mount of Olives should also not go unobserved. The fact is that there is no effort on the part of Jesus to keep his messiahship secret – certainly not in Mark's narrative, for Mark's narrative, and, I would add, the historical event, can only be construed as a clear assertion of a kind of messiahship.

The fourth incident I want to fasten on to is the trial and condemnation of Jesus. That Jesus was found guilty of claiming to be King of the Jews is the testimony of all four Gospels (Mark 15:26; Matt. 27:37; Luke 23:38; John 19:19). The frequent repetition of the title in Mark 15 – vv. 2, 9, 12, 26, 32 – is particularly noticeable. Since it was not a title employed by the early Church there can be little doubt, Bultmann notwithstanding, that we are on sure historical ground here: Jesus was crucified as a messianic pretender, because of the political connotations of the title King of the Jews. But this implies that there was some basis to the charge and the condemnation – that there were substantial grounds for applying it to Jesus – that, indeed, the title was in some sense accepted by him. The historicity of the trial scene in 15:2ff inevitably reflects favourably on the authenticity of the earlier hearing described in 14:55ff, since it can be fairly argued that the question of Pilate (15:2) is simply the Graeco–Roman version of the question of the high priest (14:61) – the blasphemy charge suitably nuanced for a Roman court.

Turning to that earlier hearing, the presumption is strong that Jesus did actually speak the words about building the Temple, in some form at least. Although Lohmeyer is probably correct in classifying *cheiropoiēton* and *acheiropoiēton* as a Marcan or community explanatory addition,[7] nevertheless the fact cannot be ignored that six NT passages testify to the saying (Mark 14:58; 15:29; Matt. 26:61; 27:40; John 2:19; Acts 6:14); and if the saying sometimes seems obscure that speaks rather in favour of than against its authenticity. Incidentally, the saying also attests to the power which was ascribed to Jesus – *katalusō*. It is not without relevance to the question we are studying that such power could be ascribed to Jesus by way of accusation – and it certainly testifies to some claim, by word or action, to messianic activity and power. As attributed to Jesus by the witnesses it can only be intended and understood messianically. The probability is high that it provided the basis of the prosecution's attack on Jesus, and Otto Betz in particular has shown how naturally an examination at that point leads on to the direct question of the high priest: "Are you the Messiah, the Son of the Blessed?"[8] – for the building of the Temple belonged to the messianic age (1 Enoch 90:29; 4 Ezra 9:38—10:27; cf. Ezek. 40—48; Jub. 1:17, 27f) and the saying involves a claim to fulfil the prophecy of Nathan (2 Sam. 7:12–14) and so to be Messiah, Son of David, and Son of God.

If we can find no adequate reason to dispute the authenticity of the course of questioning, what are we to make of Jesus' reply to the high priest's question? It is here that Wrede's thesis breaks down completely. For however affirmative or evasive were his opening words – and we shall return to this point shortly – there is no doubt that the high priest understood the reply as a messianic claim: the high priest's tearing of his clothes was hardly prompted by the *silence* of Jesus. In the words of Montefiore, "We must surely believe that the Messiahship was at least ventilated, and that it was resolved that Jesus was to be denounced to Pilate on that ground."[9]

## II

Wrede's thesis that the messianic secret motif had a theological rather than a historical origin was based on his conclusion that certain elements of that motif were clearly *unhistorical*. We are now in a position to stand Wrede's line of reasoning on its head, for our conclusion thus far is that certain elements of that motif are clearly *historical*; that is, that the messianic character of the tradition is not the reflection of post-resurrection Christian theology – it belongs to the incidents themselves. On the basis of *that* conclusion we can now present the thesis that contrary to Wrede the so-called "messianic secret" motif had a historical rather than theological origin. To argue this thesis in depth is beyond the scope of this paper, but the four incidents already examined almost constitute proof enough.

First the feeding of the five thousand. The important points which emerge here are first: that there was abroad, in Galilee at least, a popular conception of the Messiah as a political kingly figure – the sort of King of the Jews that Pilate felt justified in crucifying; that Jesus was a Messiah of this type was the conclusion reached by those whom Jesus miraculously fed in the desert. The second important point is the evidence of how Jesus reacted against this attempt to force a false messianic role on him. He saw all too clearly how politically inflammable the Galilean crowd was. The lesson learned, or confirmed, by this effect of his display of authority would go a long way towards explaining his reticence in other situations.

With regard to Peter's confession, the interesting thing is again Jesus' reaction. Peter hails him as Messiah; and how does Jesus respond? There is certainly no question of his denying the title – but there is also no indication of his accepting it beyond the impersonal *peri autou* of 8:30. 8:30 is a word neither of rebuke nor of congratulation. It is a command to silence followed immediately by explicit and very pointed teaching about the nature of his messiahship. The implication is strong that Peter was little further forward than the Galilean crowd in his understanding of Jesus' messiahship. The command to silence is given not so much because Jesus' messiahship is secret, but because it is misunderstood.

In the entry into Jerusalem three points call for attention. The first is that Mark carefully avoids making the messianic character of the event fully explicit. The Zechariah prophecy is not referred to; the ovation seems to come from the disciples rather than the crowd, and the cries of welcome fall short of complete messianic recognition and homage. The second is the manner of Jesus' entry: he comes as the humble king who speaks peace, not as the political King of the Jews. The third is the fact that the authorities did not immediately pull Jesus in and that no reference seems to have been made to the entry at the trial – which suggests that no political significance was seen or could easily be read into the entry. In short, Jesus' entry into Jerusalem was an enacted parable about the nature of his messiahship. Those whose ears were attuned to catch political overtones heard nothing. Those who looked and listened for the coming of the Kingdom saw something of eschatological and messianic significance, but fell short of full understanding.

In the trial of Jesus once again interest centres on Jesus' response to the questions put to him by the high priest and by Pilate. I am much impressed by the arguments in favour of the longer reading in 14:62. What scribe faced by the triumphant and unequivocal *egō eimi* would dilute it to the colourless and equivocal *su eipas hoti egō eimi*? And the longer reading certainly accounts for the texts of Matthew and Luke. In that case Jesus' reply to the high priest is very similar to his reply to Pilate. To both questions – "Are you the Christ?" and "Are you the King of the Jews?" – Jesus answers in effect, "You could put it that way." He accepts the titles, but at the same time makes it clear that he does not attach the same significance to them as do his questioners (cf. John 18:33–7). These exchanges are important in that they exemplify the dilemma which must constantly have confronted Jesus – could he accept or use *simpliciter* titles which meant one thing to himself and something very different to his hearers?

The conclusions I draw from studying these passages are that Jesus believed himself to be Messiah, but that his conception of the messianic role was an unexpected and unpopular one. Because the title Messiah had such different connotations to Jesus and to those who heard him he never used it of himself or unequivocally welcomed its application to him by others; and when his actions or words seemed to encourage the to him false conception of messiahship he tried to prevent it by commands to silence. Nevertheless he did not deny his right to the title, but attempted to re-educate his hearers in the significance of it for him. And the claims he made to messiahship and messianic authority were of a parabolic sort whose significance was there, plain for all to see whose eyes were not blinded and whose ears were not clogged by misconceptions (8:17–21).

These conclusions follow directly from the four passages we examined. But I believe that they hold true for the whole of the Marcan tradition, and to round off the argument I will merely illustrate the force of this contention by drawing attention to three other motifs which shed light over the whole Gospel. First of all, the motif of authoritative teaching and action. I refer in particular to the section 2:1–3:6. We have four very definite claims made by Jesus to very considerable status and authority – authority to forgive sins (2:10), authority to command and call (*kalesai*) people (2:14, 17), status as bridegroom (2:19 – in the context of OT thought a very pointed and meaningful metaphor) and status and authority as Lord over the sabbath (2:27f.; 3:4–6). In none of these incidents could it be said that Jesus was explicitly claiming to be Messiah, but in each case there were messianic overtones – overtones which the individual seeking the truth would be able to recognize.

Secondly, there is the parabolic nature of Jesus' teaching to which attention is drawn in chap. 4. I would draw attention again to the *ta panta* in 4:11: "to you has been given the mystery of the Kingdom, but to those outside all things are in parables", or, as Jeremias translates, "all things are obscure". Bearing in mind 4:33f, I take the parallelism of this verse to signify that *all* Jesus' teaching was in the nature of a parable; that is, to those who had ears to hear (4:9) the parable unfolded its meaning; but to those whose ears were dulled to the note of divine authority the parable gave no light.[10] I have no doubt that this double-edged quality of Jesus' teaching was his own choice. Rather than a straightforward statement of certain truths which would register on most of his hearers' understanding but make no impact on their emotions or their will, Jesus deliberately chose to speak in parables so that the truth thus conveyed might have maximum impact, even if only on a few.

Thirdly, I would point to the phrase "Son of man", the self-designation preferred by Jesus, as I believe it to be. Again we enter a much-ploughed field, and I will not attempt to plough a fresh furrow. Suffice it to say that the work of Geza Vermes on the one hand, and of Morna Hooker on the other, serve to underline how fully that phrase exemplifies the parabolic nature of Jesus' messianic claims. Vermes cites several examples of Aramaic usage which seem to support the view that *bar nash*(*a*) could have been used by Jesus as a circumlocution for "I", and that the phrase could have been understood by his hearers in that sense.[11] Nor can the link between the Marcan Son of Man and thc Danielic Son of Man so well forged by Miss Hooker be easily broken.[12] In the words of Matthew Black: "No term was more fitted both to conceal, yet at the same time to reveal to those who had ears to hear, the Son of Man's real identity."[13]

Finally, attention should also be drawn to the parallel noted by Richard Longenecker between the synoptic Jesus on the one hand and the Qumran Teacher of Righteousness and Simeon ben Kosebah on the other. Common features in each case include (1) external acclamation, (2) reticence on the part of the individual to speak of himself in terms used of him by others, and (3) consciousness on that individual's part of the ultimate validity of the titles employed. The basis of this common pattern Longenecker finds not in any "messianic secret" theology, but in the Jewish view that "no man can be defined as a messiah before he has accomplished the task of the anointed". If this is so it certainly enhances the historicity of the synoptic picture.

In short, I believe that to speak of a messianic *secret* is misleading and unjustified. So far as Jesus' messiahship was concerned there was no secret as such, only a cautious disavowal of false views – those of the Galilean wonder-worker and of the warrior or political King of the Jews – and an equally cautious assertion and explication of his own understanding of messiahship – that of service and suffering in this world and of exaltation only after death. As to the reason for this, all the evangelists agree: Jesus was indeed Messiah during his earthly life, but his messiahship was incomplete and inevitably misunderstood during that phase. Only with the cross, resurrection and exaltation would he enter into the fullness of his messianic office, and only then could its true nature be properly understood by men. The so-called secrecy motif in Mark is nothing other than *Mark's* method of bringing home to his readers *the programmatic nature of Jesus' messiahship.*

Wrede's thesis has been subjected to many criticisms in the course of its life, and the recent attempts to defend and define its *raison d'être* must be pronounced inadequate. Since the "messianic secret" motif is part and parcel of the tradition itself we are at the end of the day more or less shut up to the choice between the mere "that"-ness of complete Bultmannian scepticism and a Jesus who was a secret or rather a misunderstood Messiah.

I do not want to overstate my case. I would not deny, for example, that Mark may have interpreted simple commands to silence demons in terms of the "messianic secret" motif (1:34; 3:11f) or that it is Mark's own opinion about the disciples which is being expressed in passages like 6:51–2; 14:40b. But the question is whether this interpretation and opinion expresses an understanding of the material which is essentially foreign to it, or whether it is merely developing a theme which is already native to the material. When one takes into account the complexity of the secrecy motif (which reflects the complexity of life) the counterbalancing publicity–revelation theme, the inherent messianic character of the pericope we examined, and the very strong probability which emerged from that examination that there were two understandings of messiahship at issue, I cannot but conclude that the so-called "messianic secret" originated in the life-situation of Jesus and is in essence at least wholly historical.

## NOTES

1 E. Schweizer, p. 66 here.

2 J. C. O'Neill, "The Silence of Jesus", *NTS* 15 (1968–9) 163f.

3 Grundmann, 1973, 167.

4 Taylor, 1952, 452.

5 Taylor, 1952, 452.

6 Nineham, 1963, 292.

7 Lohmeyer, 1963, 326.

8 O. Betz, "Die Frage nach dem messianischen Bewusstsein Jesu", *NovT* 6 (1963) 24–37.

9 C. G. Montefiore, *The Synoptic Gospels* [2] (London: Macmillan, 1927), i, 357.

10 The saying has to be read together with those of vv. 21–2, as the repetition of

the challenge to hear aright makes clear (4:9, 23). Jesus came to give light, and his teaching shed light enough; nevertheless that light was hidden for many, and would remain so for the time being, till either the resurrection or the parousia.

11 G. Vermes in an appendix to M. Black, *An Aramaic Approach to the Gospels and Acts* (Oxford: Clarendon Press, 1967) 310–28; although see J. A. Fitzmyer's critical review in *CBQ* 30 (1968) 424–8.

12 M. Hooker, *The Son of Man in Mark* (London: SPCK, 1967).

13 Black, 329; see also I. H. Marshall, "The Synoptic Son of Man Sayings in Recent Discussion", *NTS* 12 (1965–6) 350f; cf. Sjöberg, 1955, 126; O'Neill, 161.

# 9
# *The "Messianic Secret" in Mark's Gospel**

HEIKKI RÄISÄNEN

## 1 *The question of the unity of the secrecy theology*

Wrede's study brought to prominence the basic question of whether the theological viewpoint of Mark's Gospel is based on a *single* secrecy theology. After the analysis undertaken here, the answer must be in the *negative*. Indeed it is not enough to separate from the secrecy theology the "contradictions" which were also identified by Wrede.[1] It has transpired that even the material assembled by Wrede does *not* present the homogeneous unity that he and most exegetes have thought.

(*a*) Of the motifs which were closely linked by Wrede, only *the commands to silence addressed to the demons and those addressed to the disciples* belong closely together. One may say that these two motifs constitute the *real* "messianic secret". The secret concerns Jesus' nature, or identity: the fact that he is the "Son of God" or the "Christ" must be kept secret. These commands to silence are not disobeyed.

(*b*) The motif of the *secret healings* should be distinguished from the real messianic secret. Jesus often (but not always) forbids those who have been healed to make known what has happened. These commands are often disobeyed. In this context, the stress lies on the fact that Jesus' miraculous deeds cannot remain hidden. This aspect within Mark's Gospel was correctly stressed by Ebeling. His mistake was to generalize this aspect, and to believe that the whole secrecy theme could be explained by it. Ulrich Luz deserves credit for having separated the miracle secret from the messianic secret in showing that, on the whole, Ebeling's interpretation explains the

* First published in *Das "Messiasgeheimnis" im Markusevangelium* by H. Räisänen (1976) 159–68. Translated by C. M. Tuckett.

former quite easily. However, the healing-, or miracle-secret does not constitute a completely unified whole. Ebeling's (and Luz's) interpretation does not fit those commands which are obeyed (5:43; 8:26). It is here that another motif (which also appears elsewhere in Mark) comes into play: Jesus seeks to avoid those interruptions which bring with them all too much publicity. (It is quite clear that this motif is somewhat discordant with what has just been said.)

(*c*) The *parable theory* should be clearly separated from the messianic secret. 4:11f remains an alien element in Mark. The idea found in these verses is not repeated elsewhere. Behind it there probably lies the experience of the negative attitude of the Jews to the gospel message. The parable theory has constituted the firmest basis for the apologetic interpretation of the messianic secret (Dibelius, Burkill). But when it is separated from the real messianic secret, then that interpretation loses much of its support.

(*d*) The motif of the *disciples' lack of understanding* clearly has a point of contact with the messianic secret in that the lack of understanding concerns first of all the identity of Jesus. But apart from this it is difficult to link the two themes very closely together. The motif of lack of understanding does not require that of the messianic secret: it can make do very well without it, as can be seen from the Fourth Gospel. The theme of the disciples' lack of understanding in Mark seems to be tied up with a contemporary, paraenetic concern, and there is scarcely any trace of this in other passages connected with the secrecy motif.

(*e*) When the secrecy concept is in this way broken down into parts which are only relatively loosely connected with each other, it becomes less surprising that the secrecy theme is completely absent from some stories. Many parts of the Gospel, e.g. the second chapter, are dominated much more by the motif of *publicity*. Cadbury and Morton Smith were clearly on the right track when they remarked that Mark's Gospel reflects the variety of the oral tradition.[2] Different motifs intersect in Mark's Gospel; individual stories, and perhaps even whole collections (2:1ff!), each have their own aims. Yet the tension between different motifs does not arise solely from the diversity of the traditions. Even within the evangelist's redactional activity there are contradictory tendencies. (E.g. the mystery of Jesus is not hidden from his opponents.)

2 *The question of the relationship between tradition and redaction*

*The real messianic secret* (in the narrow sense defined above) *is a redactional construction of the evangelist*. The commands to silence addressed to the demons (1:34; 3:12) as well as the command to the disciples at Caesarea Philippi (8:30) go back to Mark. However, in building up this construction, Mark was able to take up seeds which were already present in the tradition.[3] In the case of the command to silence on the descent from the mountain of the transfiguration (9:9), only three disciples are given a command, and this is for a fixed time and only concerns one special case; in all probability this should be taken as part of the tradition. In 8:30 Mark appears to have *generalized* this command: all the disciples are now bound to secrecy; the secret concerns Jesus' nature and identity as a whole; also, any time limit disappears. The commands to the demons are equally general and without limit. Here too Mark's tradition gave him a starting-point (1:25) in that it related how, in the case of a demon who had addressed Jesus as the "holy one of God", Jesus had spoken sternly and silenced it. Of course, in the tradition, this kind of action did not involve any secrecy about Jesus' identity: rather, it formed part of the exorcism. But Mark interpreted the story with his own point of view in mind, as 1:32–4 and 3:11f show.

Over and above this, other traditional statements, which in various ways placed a veil of mystery about Jesus, were fed into the Marcan view of the secret. The tradition knew how Jesus sometimes withdrew into solitude, how he healed some people in private or in the presence of only a chosen few, etc. The idea of the "miracle secret" (the command not to make the healing known in 8:26, perhaps also 5:43) appears to have been already present in the tradition. All that could have influenced the real Marcan messianic secret. However, the latter clearly presents a reinterpretation of the tradition. On the other hand, Mark developed the idea of the miracle secret in a different direction from that of the messianic secret, so that the stress now lies on the disobeying of the command and the ensuing publicity (7:36). This motif too was at his disposal in the tradition (1:45, cf. Matt. 9:30f).[4]

The tradition also knew of the disciples' lack of understanding and of their improper behaviour on many occasions. Mark brought this idea sharply into focus. The parable theory also stems from the tradition, but Mark did not develop it further. Neither of these two motifs has any direct significance for the real messianic secret.

### 3 *The question of the interpretation of the real messianic secret*

What has been said above is an attempt to determine *what* Mark has done: *how* he used and interpreted the tradition, and what new features he introduced into the total picture. But now as ever the question remains unanswered as to *why* Mark proceeded in this way.

Why did Mark develop his own special construction of the (real) messianic secret out of various traditional elements?

This question seems to lead to some frustration. For all that Mark's book has been thoroughly examined during the last decade, the statement with which U. Luz started his article ten years ago still seems to be valid: "The messianic secret is still a mystery."[5] Whoever claims to know precisely what Mark was aiming at with his secrecy theory is probably over-reaching himself. Mark gives no direct indication, and the only remaining method, i.e. reading between the lines, carries with it considerable possibilities for error. One can thus do little more here than give a final review of the most important interpretations of the secret in the light of the analysis undertaken above.

(*a*) *Wrede's* interpretation. With regard to Wrede's four basic tenets we can say this. First, the motifs linked by Wrede cannot be explained as an unbroken whole (against Wrede). From this it follows, secondly, that the key offered by Wrede (9:9) cannot open all the doors. There is still the question of whether this verse might nevertheless provide the solution to the problem of the real messianic secret. But this is difficult to maintain since 9:9 probably stems from the tradition. Whether this verse can then be used as the basis for the interpretation of *Mark's* redactional construction is at least questionable, the more so since 15:39, which rather contradicts it, *might* be Marcan. I shall have to return to this question in discussing the "history of revelation" interpretation.

According to Wrede, the messianic secret was not an idea which was first created by Mark; this was his third tenet. This view has not been supported by our analysis. The real messianic secret is to be ascribed to the evangelist. Consequently, Wrede's fourth tenet, i.e. his view about the origin of the secrecy idea, is also untenable.[6] Thus all Wrede's basic tenets have been shown to need correction. This does not of course alter the fact that the impetus given by Wrede has been, and still is, of decisive importance for the interpretation of Mark.

(*b*) The *apologetic* interpretation. The breaking up of the secrecy complex into separate parts seems at first sight to remove some of the difficulties associated with this theory. The publicizing of some miracles is not a decisive objection to this theory if the miracle secret is to be separated from the real messianic secret. Further, the apologetic theory no longer completely comes to grief on the fact that the disciples' failure to understand originates in their obduracy, if the lack of understanding motif is no longer intrinsically linked with the real messianic secret. But there are still problems for this interpretation, since the parable theory must also be excluded from the context of the messianic secret. Certainly the parable theory concerns the problem of the Jews, but the messianic secret is not to be interpreted in relation to this. That does not mean that the apologetic theory is absolutely impossible. It is simply that it has lost its most important positive basis. A further weakness is the fact that, according to this interpretation, the messianic secret remains a "subsidiary concept", which the evangelist uses to reply to specific objections from outsiders. It is somewhat difficult to believe that the secrecy theory does not have a positive significance of its own.

(*c*) The *epiphany* interpretation. The merits of Ebeling's interpretation have been noted in this chapter too. Practically the whole of the miracle secret can be explained in this way without difficulty. On the other hand, this interpretation cannot explain the real messianic secret, unless the commands to silence addressed to the demons and the disciples are interpreted away as purely literary and symbolic references to the reader.

(*d*) The "*theology of the cross*" interpretation. The breaking up of the secrecy complex removes some obstacles in the way of this interpretation too. There is no longer any need to try to interpret the miracle secret in the light of the theology of the cross in an artificial way. Also 9:9 (where the resurrection, rather than the cross, marks the central point) need not be a stumbling-block if the verse is traditional and does not represent Mark's view completely. It is also undisputed that the theology of the cross does justice to a central feature in Mark's theology.

But it is another matter how the theology of suffering in Mark is connected with the secrecy idea in particular. Even the removal of all the commands to silence from the Gospel would hardly detract significantly from Mark's theology of the cross! Also, the "theology of the cross" interpretation assumes that the commands to silence are to be understood primarily as symbolic references for the reader. Added to this, finally, is the fact that in 3:12 it is the majesty of Jesus which is hidden.

Accordingly, the secrecy idea cannot be seen as correcting a *theios anēr* Christology. That is not the meaning of Mark's cross-centred theology when this is separated from the messianic secret either. Mark's Jesus is a *theios anēr* even at his death.[7] In speaking of his suffering, Jesus' sovereign knowledge about the future is brought clearly into prominence. A theology of suffering and a *theios anēr*

Christology are in no way mutually exclusive for Mark. Their mutual exclusion is due to modern wishful thinking.

(*e*) The "*history of revelation*" interpretation. Again the breaking up of the secrecy motif removes some difficulties. If the miracle secret is a separate motif, then the publicizing of the miracles before Easter is no longer fatal to the theory. The difficulty of the fact that the disciples' total lack of understanding ends long before Easter is perhaps also not too serious, if the lack of understanding motif cannot be linked very closely with the messianic secret. Certain problems arise, however, from the fact that 9:9 constitutes the cornerstone of this theory, an inheritance from Wrede. Here the resurrection is explicitly mentioned as the moment when the secret ends. As was stressed earlier, however, this verse mentions only one individual case and therefore seems to be traditional. On the other hand, one could claim that precisely this saying seems to have provided a starting-point for the redactional secrecy theology; did it perhaps even give rise to the theory? Has Mark then silently generalized the time limit of 9:9 (the resurrection), so that in his view it applies to the whole of the real messianic secret?

15:39 presents difficulties for this hypothesis. It is a verse which may have been added by Mark. In the light of this saying, it seems that one can only advocate the periodization of history which this interpretation presupposes in a modified way, i.e. so that the resurrection is not particularly stressed. If Mark has indeed generalized the *terminus ad quem* implied in 9:9, then he has also made it less precise and blurred the line between crucifixion and resurrection. The death and resurrection of Jesus would then *together* constitute the decisive watershed between hiddenness and openness.

It must be conceded that it is difficult to find any really positive point of support for the "history of revelation" interpretation (unless it be 15:39) – that is, after 9:9 is questioned as evidence for Mark's redaction. Nevertheless, it seems to me that *the "history of revelation" interpretation in modified form is least beset with difficulties* as an explanation of the messianic secret. But note that this is as an explanation of the *real* messianic secret (and not of the whole complex which Wrede suggested, as Percy and Strecker suppose).

It seems to have been an important idea for Mark that something fundamental about Jesus was evident only *after* his earthly activity. A real christological confession is only possible in the new situation created by Jesus' death and resurrection – in the situation where Jesus acts as the exalted Lord.[8] In the new circumstances one understands things which were previously beyond one's grasp. Things which were hidden from of old have now been revealed to the saints. These include, above all, Christ, the mystery of God "in whom all the treasures of wisdom and knowledge lie hidden" (Col. 2:2f).[9] We may speculate a little further. Against this background, the fact that the tradition about Jesus contained christological sayings, even in the form of open confessions of faith during Jesus' lifetime, must have been a difficulty for the evangelist. One could not eliminate them. But Mark stressed that the situation was exceptional. The closest companions of Jesus were in a special position. By God's grace they learnt the fundamental truth before it was possible for others. For these others, things *had* to remain hidden. That is how Jesus must have intended it. But he had also (as Mark knew from the tradition) forbidden the transfiguration to be made known. It was similar with the demons who, as spiritual beings, were capable of knowing more than human beings.

Mark therefore intervened in his traditions whenever the community's christological confession was about to be heard "prematurely". He wanted to make clear that this confession was really only possible in the new period of salvation history. Of course the reader could have expected much more consistency from him. Mark seems to have intervened only where Jesus was acclaimed Son of God or something similar in the form of a quite direct "You are" or "I know you". No explanation of the secrecy motif can remove the tension which exists in the Gospel between secrecy and openness. The reader inevitably gets the impression from Mark's work that Jesus in no way kept his identity hidden in every situation, and that some outsiders like Bartimaeus could be clear about it. Mark might have been able to resolve part of this inconsistency by being more skilful in his redactional technique. However, openness plays so great a role in his material that it would not have been possible to remove it completely. The contradictions in the motif thus stem on the one hand from mutually contradictory traditions, but on the other hand from the unsystematic nature of Mark's redactional work. Mark can of his own accord stress the idea of openness redactionally where this fits his own (perhaps polemical) aims. The way the disciples appear in many, somewhat diverse, roles would also be comparable with this phenomenon.[10]

4 Even this modified "history of revelation" interpretation of the commands to silence to the demons and the disciples is not completely satisfactory. It does not matter to me very much whether it is accepted or not. The conclusions about the nature of Mark's

redaction overall, to which the analysis of the secrecy problem has given rise, appear to me far more important. Classic form criticism saw in Mark a bearer and collector of traditions with a few ideas of his own. Modern redaction criticism has made him into an important, original and independent theological thinker. In my view the new picture urgently needs correcting. If the analysis presented in this book is on the right lines, then the pendulum will have to swing back to the older position – perhaps to stop half way. Certainly Mark has his own theological ideas; certainly he presents some new nuances of his own. But a complete, unified picture of his theology which is in any way satisfactory can scarcely be attained without forcing the evidence. One must therefore be content to see the earliest evangelist as more of a bearer of tradition, and less of a theologian or interpreter, than recent research has generally assumed him to be.

## NOTES

(Some extra notes have been added to clarify some of the cross-references made by Räisänen to earlier parts of his book. These have been enclosed in square brackets.)

1 [Cf. Räisänen, 1976, 143ff. See also Wrede, 1971, 124ff, and the introduction in this volume, p. 5 above.]

2 [Räisänen earlier (48) cited the remarks of H. J. Cadbury, "Mixed Motives in the Gospels", *Proceedings of the American Philosophical Society* 95 (1951) 119f: "If he [Mark] had any purpose of his own it is either parallel to that of his material or not distinctive enough to be conspicuous amid the medley of motifs and motives in his material ... The material marshalled for the theory [the messianic secret] seems to me to represent several quite different motives instead of a single one." Also M. Smith, "Comments on Taylor's Commentary on Mark", *HTR* 48 (1955), 21–64, on p. 29: "Actually, the early Church had a wide variety of motives for attributing secret doctrine to Jesus ... Every such attribution, therefore, must be judged individually."]

3 This is the answer to Wrede's question of how Mark could have introduced a new secrecy idea into his book [cf. Wrede, 1971, 145]. The idea was only *partly* new.

4 [Räisänen earlier (66ff) argued that Matt. 9:30f may represent an independent tradition, rather than being a Matthean redactional construction, as is usually assumed: despite the Matthean language and style, the presence of the secrecy motif seems somewhat alien to Matthew's own redactional interests (e.g. his stress on the value of faith).]

5 Luz, p. 75 in this volume.

6 Wrede's critics are right in saying that the tradition gives no trace of an "unmessianic" view of the earthly life of Jesus. [Räisänen also refers here to

an earlier point in his book (33 n. 1) where he endorses Strecker's argument against Wrede's theory on this point (see p. 54 in this volume).]

7 [Earlier (157) Räisänen argued this on the grounds that the centurion's confession may be a response to the miracles occurring at the time of Jesus' death (e.g. the darkness).]

8 See Strecker (p. 62 in this volume); the messianic secret "is an essential expression of a theology of salvation history. Its goal is the time after the resurrection; it implies the christological recognition that the story of the earthly Jesus does not remain on its own but points to his enthronement as Lord." On the other hand, Percy, 1953, 294f, places too much stress on the alleged similarity between Mark's viewpoint and Paul's theology, whereby the period prior to the resurrection would be also for Mark "only a period of humility and therefore also of secrecy". This is not the case; openness plays all too great a role in Mark's Gospel. No doubt the earthly life of Jesus only constitutes the prelude to the real "gospel" of the heavenly Lord – but the tone is still the same.

9 Strecker (pp. 62f in this volume) correctly stresses the ecclesiological background of the secrecy theology. Mark's community possesses "remarkable self-awareness".

10 [Räisänen earlier argued that the disciples have various positive roles in Mark, e.g. as mediators of the tradition (cf. 9:28f; 13:3ff) (56), as examples for discipleship (1:16–20) or as representatives of later Christian missionaries (6:7ff) (136).]

# *Bibliography*

Ambrozic, A. M. *The Hidden Kingdom. A Redaction–Critical Study of the References to the Kingdom of God in Mark's Gospel.* Washington, D.C.: Catholic Biblical Association, 1972.

Aune, D. E. "The Problem of the Messianic Secret", *NovT* 11 (1969) 1–31.

Barbour, R. S. "Recent Study of the Gospel according to St Mark", *ExpT* 79 (1968) 324–9.

Best, E. "The Role of the Disciples in Mark", *NTS* 23 (1977) 377–401.

Betz, H. D. "Jesus as Divine Man", in F. T. Trotter (ed.), *Jesus and the Historian* (Festschrift for E. C. Colwell. Philadelphia: Westminster, 1968) 114–33.

Bickermann, E. "Das Messiasgeheimnis und die Komposition des Markusevangeliums", *ZNW* 22 (1923) 122–40.

Blevins, J. L. *The Messianic Secret in Markan Research 1901–1964*. Ph.D. thesis, Southern Baptist Theological Seminary, 1965.

Boobyer, G. H. "The Secrecy Motif in St Mark's Gospel", *NTS* 6 (1960) 225–35.

Bousset, W. *Jesus*. ET London: Williams & Norgate; New York: Putnam's, 1906 (German 1904).

—*Kyrios Christos*. ET of 2nd 1921 edn. New York: Abingdon, 1970.

Brown, S. "The Secret of the Kingdom of God (Mark 4:11)", *JBL* 92 (1973) 60–74.

Bultmann, R. "Die Frage nach dem messianischen Bewusstsein Jesu und das Petrus-Bekenntnis", *ZNW* 19 (1919/20) 165–74 (= *Exegetica* [Tübingen: Mohr, 1967] 1–9).

—*The Theology of the New Testament I*. ET New York: Charles Schribner's Sons, 1951; London: SCM, 1952 (German 1949).

—*The History of the Synoptic Tradition*. ET of 2nd 1931 edn and 1958 supp. Oxford: Blackwell; New York: Harper & Row, 1963, rev. 1968. (First German edn, 1921).

—"The New Approach to the Synoptic Problem", *Existence and Faith* (London: Collins, 1964) 39–62.

Burkill, T. A. "The Hidden Son of Man in St. Mark's Gospel", *ZNW* 52 (1961) 189–213.

—*Mysterious Revelation*. Ithaca, New York: Cornell University, 1963. (See pp. 44–8 in this volume.)

Clark, J. L. *A Re-examination of the Problem of the Messianic Secret in its Relationship to the Synoptic Son of Man Sayings*. Ph.D. thesis, Yale University, 1962.

Conzelmann, H. "Present and Future in the Synoptic Tradition", *Journal*

*for Theology and the Church* 5 (1968) 26–44 (German in *ZTK* 54 (1957) 277–96).
—*An Outline of the Theology of the New Testament*. ET London: SCM; New York: Harper & Row, 1969 (German 1968).
—"History and Theology in the Passion Narratives of the Synoptic Gospels", *Int* 24 (1970) 178–97.
Dahl, N. A. "The Purpose of Mark's Gospel", *Jesus in the Memory of the Early Church* (Minneapolis: Augsburg, 1976) 52–65 (Swedish 1958). (See pp. 29–34 in this volume.)
Dibelius, M. *From Tradition to Gospel*. ET New York: Charles Scribner's Sons; London: Ivor Nicholson & Watson, 1934 (First German edn, 1919).
Dunn, J. D. G. "The Messianic Secret in Mark", *Tyndale Bulletin* 21 (1970) 92–117. (See pp. 116–31 in this volume).
Ebeling, H. J. *Das Messiasgeheimnis und die Botschaft des Marcus-Evangelisten*. Berlin: A. Töpelmann, 1939.
Focant, C. "L'incompréhension des disciples dans le deuxième évangile", *RB* 83 (1975) 161–85.
Fuller, R. H. *The New Testament in Current Study*. London: SCM; New York: Charles Scribner's Sons, 1963.
—*The Foundations of New Testament Christology*. London: Lutterworth; New York: Charles Scribner's Sons, 1965.
Glasswell, M. E. *The Concealed Messiahship in the Synoptic Gospels and the Significance of this for the Study of the Life of Jesus and of the Early Church*. Ph.D. thesis, Durham University, 1965.
—"The Use of Miracles in the Markan Gospel", in C. F. D. Moule (ed.), *Miracles* (London: Mowbrays, 1965) 151–62.
—"St Mark's Attitude to the Relationship between History and the Gospel", in E. A. Livingstone (ed.), *Studia Biblica* (*1978*) *II* (Sheffield; *JSOT*, 1980) 115–27.
Grant, F. C. *The Earliest Gospel*. New York: Abingdon, 1943.
Grundmann, W. *Das Evangelium nach Markus*. Berlin: Evangelische Verlagsanstalt, [6]1973.
Haenchen, E. *Der Weg Jesu*. Berlin: De Gruyter, [2]1968.
Hawkin, D. J. "The Incomprehension of the Disciples in the Markan Redaction", *JBL* 91 (1972) 491–500.
Hay, L. S. "Mark's Use of the Messianic Secret", *Journal of the American Academy of Religion* 35 (1967) 16–27.
Horstmann, M. *Studien zur markinischen Christologie*. Münster: Aschendorff, 1969.
Jülicher, A. *Neue Linien in der Kritik der evangelischen Überlieferung*. Giessen: A. Töpelmann, 1906.
Keck, L. E. "The Introduction to Mark's Gospel", *NTS* 12 (1966) 352–70.
Kee, H. C. *Community of the New Age*. London: SCM; Philadelphia: Westminster, 1977.
Kelber, W. H. *The Kingdom in Mark*. Philadelphia: Fortress, 1974.
Kermode, F. *The Sense of an Ending*. New York: Oxford University, 1967.

—*The Genesis of Secrecy*. Cambridge, Mass., and London: Harvard University, 1979.

Kertelge, K. *Die Wunder Jesu im Markusevangelium*. München: Kosel, 1970.

Koch, D. A. *Die Bedeutung der Wundererzählungen für die Christologie des Markusevangeliums*. Berlin: De Gruyter, 1975.

Koester, H. "One Jesus and Four Primitive Gospels", in J. M. Robinson, H. Koester, *Trajectories through Early Christianity* (Philadelphia: Fortress, 1971) 158–204.

Kuby, A. "Zur Konzeption des Marcus-Evangeliums", *ZNW* 49 (1958) 52–64.

Kuhn, H.-W. *Ältere Sammlungen im Markusevangelium*. Göttingen: Vandenhoek & Ruprecht, 1971.

Lambrecht, J. "The Christology of Mark", *Biblical Theology Bulletin* 3 (1973) 256–73.

Lightfoot, R. H. *History and Interpretation in the Gospels*. London: Hodder & Stoughton; New York: Harper & Brothers, 1935.

Lohmeyer, E. *Das Evangelium des Markus*. Göttingen: Vandenhoek & Ruprecht, [16]1963.

Longenecker, R. N. "The Messianic Secret in the Light of Recent Discoveries", *EvQ* 41 (1969) 207–15.

Luz, U. "Das Geheimnismotiv und die markinische Christologie", *ZNW* 56 (1965) 9–30. (See pp. 75–96 in this volume.)

Manson, T. W. "Realised Eschatology and the Messianic Secret", in D. E. Nineham (ed.), *Studies in the Gospels* (Essays in Memory of R. H. Lightfoot. Oxford: Blackwell, 1955), 209–22.

Marxsen, W. *Introduction to the New Testament*. ET Oxford: Blackwell; Philadelphia: Fortress, 1968 (German 1964).

Meye, R. P. "Messianic Secret and Messianic Didache in Mark's Gospel", in F. Christ (ed.), *OIKONOMIA* (Festschrift for O. Cullmann. Hamburg: Herbert Rich, 1967) 57–68.

Moule, C. F. D. "On Defining the Messianic Secret in Mark", in E. E. Ellis and E. Grässer (ed.), *Jesus und Paulus* (Festschrift for W. G. Kümmel. Göttingen: Vandenhoek & Ruprecht, 1975) 239–52.

Minette de Tillesse, G. *Le secret messianique dans L'Evangile de Marc*. Paris: Cerf, 1968.

Nineham, D. E. *Saint Mark*. Harmondsworth & Baltimore: Penguin, 1963.

Peake, A. S. "The Messiah and the Son of Man", *BJRL* 8 (1924) 52–81.

Percy, E. *Die Botschaft Jesu*. Lund: Gleerup, 1953.

Pesch, R. *Das Markusevangelium I & II*. Freiburg: Herder, 1976 and 1977.

Powley, B. G. "The Purpose of the Messianic Secret: A Brief Survey", *ExpTim* 80 (1969) 308–10.

—*The "Messianic Secret" in Mark's Gospel. An Historical Survey*. Ph.D. thesis, Glasgow University, 1979.

—"Vincent Taylor and the Messianic Secret in Mark's Gospel", in E. A. Livingstone (ed.), *Studia Biblica (1978) II* (Sheffield; *JSOT*, 1980) 243–6.

Räisänen, H. *Das "Messiasgeheimnis" im Markusevangelium*. Helsinki: Lansi-Suomi, 1976. (See pp. 132–40 in this volume.)

Rawlinson, A. E. J. *St. Mark*. Westminster Commentary. London: Methuen, 1925.

Robinson, J. M. *A New Quest of the Historical Jesus*. London: SCM, 1959; Missoula: Scholars Press Reprint Series 2, 1979.

—"The Recent Debate on the 'New Quest'", *Journal of Bible and Religion* 30 (1962) 198–208.

—"Gnosticism and the New Testament", in B. Aland (ed.), *Gnosis* (Festschrift for H. Jonas. Göttingen: Vandenhoek & Ruprecht, 1978) 125–43.

Robinson, W. C. "The Quest for Wrede's Secret Messiah", *Int* 27 (1973) 10–30. (See pp. 97–115 in this volume.)

Roloff, J. "Das Markusevangelium als Geschichtsdarstellung", *EvT* 29 (1969) 73–93.

Sanday, W. "The Injunctions to Silence in the Gospels", *JTS* 5 (1904) 321–9.

—*The Life of Christ in Recent Research*. Oxford: Clarendon, 1907.

—"The Apocalyptic Element in the Gospels", *Hibbert Journal* 10 (1911) 83–109.

Schmidt, K. L. *Der Rahmen der Geschichte Jesu*. Berlin: Trowitzsch & Sohn, 1919.

Schniewind, J. "Messiasgeheimnis und Eschatologie", in E. Kähler (ed.), *Nachgelassene Reden und Aufsätze* (Berlin: A. Töpelmann, 1952) 1–13.

—*Das Evangelium nach Markus*. Göttingen: Vandenhoek & Ruprecht, [10]1963.

Schreiber, J. "Die Christologie des Markusevangeliums", *ZTK* 58 (1961) 154–83.

Schweitzer, A. *The Mystery of the Kingdom of God*. ET London: Black, 1925 (German 1901).

—*The Quest of the Historical Jesus*. London: Black, [3]1954, reprinted SCM, 1980; New York: Macmillan, 1961 (First German edn 1906).

Schweizer, E. "Anmerkungen zur Theologie des Markus", *Neotestamentica* (Zurich: Zwingli, 1963) 93–104.

—"Die theologische Leistung des Markus", *EvT* 24 (1964) 337–55.

—"Mark's Contribution to the Quest of the Historical Jesus", *NTS* 10 (1964) 421–32.

—"Zur Messiasgeheimnis bei Markus", *ZNW* 56 (1965) 1–8. (See pp. 65–74 in this volume.)

—*The Good News according to Mark*. Richmond, Va.: John Knox, 1970; London: SPCK, 1971.

—"Neuere Markus-Forschung in USA", *EvT* 33 (1973) 533–7.

—"Towards a Christology of Mark", in J. Jervell and W. A. Meeks (ed.), *God's Christ and His People* (Festschrift for N. A. Dahl. Oslo: Universitetsforlahet, 1977) 29–42.

Sjöberg, E. *Der verborgene Menschensohn in den Evangelien*. Lund: Gleerup, 1955.

Strecker, G. "Zur Messiasgeheimnistheorie im Markusevangelium", *SE* 3 (TU 88. Berlin, 1964) 87–104. (See pp. 49–64 in this volume.)

Tagawa, K. *Miracle et Evangile. La pensée personelle de l'évangeliste Marc.* Paris: Presses Universitaires de France, 1966.

Taylor, V. "The Messianic Secret in Mark", *ExpTim* 59 (1948) 146–51.

—*The Gospel according to St. Mark.* London: Macmillan, 1952.

—"W. Wrede's The Messianic Secret in the Gospels", *ExpTim* 65 (1954) 246–50.

Theissen, G. *Urchristliche Wundergeschichten.* Göttingen: Gerd Mohn, 1974.

Trocmé, E. "Is there a Markan Christology?", in B. Lindars and S. S. Smalley (ed.), *Christ and Spirit in the New Testament* (Festschrift for C. F. D. Moule. Cambridge: Cambridge University, 1973) 3–13.

—*The Formation of the Gospel according to Mark.* London: SPCK; Philadelphia: Westminster, 1975 (French 1963).

Tyson, J. B. "The Blindness of the Disciples in Mark", *JBL* 80 (1961) 261–8. (See pp. 35–43 in this volume.)

Vielhauer, Ph. "Erwägungen zur Christologie des Markusevangeliums", *Aufsätze zum Neuen Testament* (Münich: Kaiser, 1965) 199–214.

Weeden, T. J. *Mark – Traditions in Conflict.* Philadelphia: Fortress, 1971.

Weiss, J. *Das älteste Evangelium.* Göttingen: Vandenhoek & Ruprecht, 1903.

Wernle, P. *The Sources of our Knowledge of the Life of Jesus.* ET London: Green, 1907.

—*Jesus.* Tübingen: Mohr, 1917.

Wrede, W. "Zur Messiaserkenntnis der Dämonen bei Markus", *ZNW* 5 (1904) 169–77.

—*The Messianic Secret.* ET London and Cambridge: James Clarke; Greenwood, S. Carolina: Attic, 1971 (German 1901).

# Index of New Testament References